The UK
Air Fryer **Cookbook** 2023

1600 Days Easy and Budget—Friendly Recipes You Will Love incl. Dinners, Sides, Snacks, Lunches & More

Tillie T. Reid

Contents

CHAPTER 3   FISH AND SEAFOOD   27

CHAPTER 4   PORK, BEEF AND LAMB

INTRODUCTION

Welcome to my new cookbook! My name is Tillie, and I'm thrilled to share my passion for air frying with you. Cooking has always been a joy for me, and I've spent countless hours in the kitchen experimenting with different recipes and techniques.

But when I first heard about air fryers, I have to admit that I was skeptical. How could you get crispy, delicious food without deep-frying it in oil? But once I tried it for myself, I was hooked. I love the speed, convenience, and versatility of air frying, and I'm excited to share my favorite recipes with you in this cookbook.

In these pages, you'll find a wide variety of recipes that are perfect for beginners. I've included classic air fryer dishes like chicken wings, french fries, and onion rings, as well as more unique recipes like jalapeño poppers, falafel, and cinnamon sugar donut holes.

But more than just a collection of recipes, this cookbook is a reflection of my own personal journey with air frying. When I first started using an air fryer, I made plenty of mistakes and had a few less-than-stellar results. But over time, I learned how to make the most of this amazing kitchen gadget, and I've included all of my best tips and tricks in these recipes.

And don't worry if you've never used an air fryer before. I've included a comprehensive guide to using an air fryer, as well as tips on how to clean and maintain it. I want this cookbook to be a valuable resource for anyone who is new to using an air fryer, and I've tried to make it as user-friendly as possible.

I've also included recipes for all kinds of occasions, from quick and easy weeknight dinners to impressive appetizers for your next party. And I've tried to keep the recipes as simple and straightforward as possible, so even if you've never used an air fryer before, you'll be able to follow along with ease.

I truly believe that air frying is a game-changer in the kitchen, and I hope that this cookbook will inspire you to try new recipes and experiment with different flavors. So let's get air frying, and let the delicious results speak for themselves!

What Are Air Fryers

An air fryer is a countertop appliance that uses hot air to cook food. It works by circulating hot air around the food at high speed, which produces a crispy and golden exterior while keeping the inside moist and tender. Air fryers typically have a heating element and a fan that work together to produce the hot air, as well as a basket or tray where the food is placed.

One of the main advantages of using an air fryer is that it requires little to no oil to cook food. Instead, the hot air circulates around the food, creating a similar result to deep-frying but with much less fat and calories. This can be a healthier option for those who want to enjoy crispy and delicious food without the added calories and fat.

Air fryers are also very versatile and can be used to cook a wide variety of foods, including meats, vegetables, frozen foods, and even baked goods. They can also be used to reheat leftovers, which can be a quick and easy way to revive dishes without using the microwave or oven.

Choosing your air fryer

When picking an air Fryer, it is important to note

the main purpose and what you would be using it for. Many things stand out for me, but I've handpicked some for you.

Capacity and Size: The size of the air fryer is important to consider, especially if you have limited counter space. Think about the size of your kitchen and how much room you have for an air fryer. The capacity of the air fryer determines how much food you can cook at one time. Think about how many people you typically cook for and choose a model that can accommodate that amount of food. If you like to meal prep, you may want to choose a larger capacity.

Power: The power of the air fryer affects how quickly and evenly it can cook your food. More powerful air fryers tend to cook food faster and more evenly, but they may also be more expensive.

Temperature range: Look for an air fryer with a wide temperature range, as this will allow you to cook a variety of foods. You want to be able to cook everything from crispy chicken to delicate fish.

Timer: A timer is a useful feature, as it allows you to set the cooking time and forget about it. Some air fryers also have an automatic shut-off feature, which is an added safety bonus.

Price: Air fryers come in a variety of price ranges, from budget-friendly to high-end models. Consider your budget and cooking needs when making your decision. Keep in mind that a higher price doesn't always mean better quality.

Features: Air fryers come with various features, such as temperature control, timer settings, and automatic shut-off. Think about which features are important to you and which ones you can do without.

Ease of use: Look for an air fryer that is easy to use and has clear instructions. Some models also have pre-programmed settings for different types of food, which can be helpful for beginners.

Ease of cleaning: Cleaning an air fryer can be a hassle, so look for models with removable parts that are dishwasher safe. This will save you time and effort when cleaning up.

Brand reputation: Choose a brand that has a good reputation for producing high-quality and reliable appliances. Read reviews from other users to get an idea of their experiences with the product.

Customer service and warranty: Look for an air fryer with a good warranty and reliable customer service. This can be helpful if you encounter any issues with the appliance.

What Can You Cook In An Air Fryer And What Foods To Avoid?

Air fryers are versatile kitchen appliances that can be used to cook a wide variety of foods.

Foods To Cook In An Air Fryer

Here are some of the different types of foods that can be cooked in an air fryer, along with some tips on how to prepare them:

French fries: Air fryers are perfect for making crispy french fries without the added oil from deep frying. Simply slice potatoes into fries, toss them in a little bit of oil and salt, and air fry them until they are crispy and golden brown.

Frozen foods: Many frozen foods, such as chicken tenders, fish sticks, and mozzarella sticks, can be cooked in an air fryer. This is a great way to get a crispy exterior without having to deep fry the food.

Fish: Air fryers are great for cooking fish, such as salmon, tilapia, and cod. Simply season the fish with herbs and spices, and air fry it until it is cooked through and crispy.

Vegetables: Air fryers are ideal for cooking vegetables, such as broccoli, Brussels sprouts, and asparagus. These can be seasoned with herbs and spices, and air fried until they are crispy and tender.

Eggs: Air fryers can be used to make scrambled eggs, omelettes, and even hard boiled eggs. Simply whisk the eggs and any desired seasonings, pour them into the air fryer basket or tray, and cook until they are set.

Foods To Avoid In An Air Fryer:

Foods that are too wet or oily: While air fryers are great for cooking crispy foods, they may not work well for foods that are too wet or oily. Examples of foods to avoid include battered fish, wet batter-coated chicken, and heavily marinated meats.

Large cuts of meat: Air fryers may not be the best choice for cooking large cuts of meat, such as roasts or whole chickens, as they may not cook evenly. The hot air circulates around the food, which can result in uneven cooking and an overcooked exterior with a undercooked interior.

Delicate foods: Foods that are delicate or easily fall apart, such as flaky fish or soft vegetables, may not work well in an air fryer. This is because the circulating hot air can cause delicate foods to break apart or become overly dried out.

Foods with sauces: Such as BBQ chicken or teriyaki chicken, can be tricky to cook in an air fryer. The sauce can cause the food to stick to the basket, resulting in an uneven cook and potentially ruining the dish.

What Are The Advantages Of Air Fryers

Air fryers are the kitchen superhero you never knew you needed! Not only do they produce delicious, crispy foods without the need for gallons of oil, but they also come with a range of other benefits that can make cooking a breeze.

1.Use Minimal Oil

Air fryers are a godsend for health-conscious cooks. With their ability to cook food with little to no oil, they can help you enjoy your favorite dishes without the added calories and fat. Plus, they make it easy to cook up a range of nutritious meals, from crispy roasted vegetables to perfectly cooked salmon.

2.Versatile

Air fryers are also super versatile, allowing you to cook all kinds of foods to perfection. Whether you're in the mood for juicy chicken wings, crunchy french fries, or a batch of fresh-baked cookies, your air fryer has got your back.

3.Less Messy

Leaning up after cooking can be a hassle, but air fryers make it a breeze. Most models have dishwasher-safe baskets and trays that can be easily popped in the dishwasher for quick and easy cleaning. And their compact size means they won't take up valuable counter space or cramp your kitchen style.

4.Time-Saving

One of the biggest advantages of air fryers is their speed. They cook food up to 25% faster than traditional ovens, which means you can enjoy your favorite meals in a fraction of the time. Plus, their convection system ensures that your food is cooked evenly and thoroughly, so you don't have to worry about any undercooked or overcooked bits.

5.Easy to Use

Safety is always a concern in the kitchen, but air fryers have got you covered. With features like automatic shut-off and cool-touch handles, you can rest assured that you're cooking in a safe and secure environment.

6.Easy to clean:

Most air fryer baskets and trays are dishwasher safe and easy to clean, which can save you time and hassle.

7.More Economical

And last but not least, air fryers are super cost-effective. Compared to other kitchen appliances, they are affordable and can help you save money in the long run.

How To Clean & Maintain Air Fryers

Allow the air fryer to cool completely and unplug it from the power source before starting the cleaning process.

Remove the air fryer basket and tray from the appliance. Empty any remaining food or debris from the basket and tray into the garbage.

If the basket and tray are dishwasher safe, place them in the dishwasher for cleaning. Otherwise, wash them in warm, soapy water using a non-abrasive sponge or cloth. Rinse thoroughly with water and dry completely before reassembling the air fryer.

Use a soft, damp cloth or sponge to wipe down the interior and exterior of the air fryer. Be careful not to get any moisture in the electrical components or the heating element.

For tough, stuck-on food or grease, you may need to use a non-abrasive sponge or brush and a mild cleaning solution to gently scrub the affected area. Avoid using harsh chemicals or abrasive materials that can damage the surface of the air fryer.

Wipe down the heating element and fan with a dry cloth to remove any grease or food residue that may have accumulated. Be sure to avoid touching the heating element with your bare hands, as it can be very hot.

Once you have finished cleaning the air fryer, reassemble the appliance and plug it back in. Run the air fryer for a few minutes to ensure that it is working properly and there is no residual moisture. Alternatively, if you want to keep your machine looking new, it's a good idea to check the air fryer's vents and filters for any blockages or buildup of debris. Clean or replace the filters as needed. In addition, inspect the power cord and plug for any signs of damage or wear. Replace the cord or appliance if necessary.

It is essential to follow the manufacturer's instructions and safety precautions when cleaning an air fryer to ensure that it remains in good working order and that there is no risk of damage or injury.

Air Fryer Safety Tips and Tricks

Cooking with an air fryer is a fun and safe way to enjoy your favorite dishes. However, it's important to follow some simple safety tips to ensure that you can cook with confidence. Here are some tips and tricks to keep in mind:

1 Place the air fryer on a stable surface to ensure it does not tilt or tip over.

2 Use oven mitts or potholders: Always use oven mitts or potholders when handling the air fryer

basket and tray, as they can become very hot during cooking.

3 Be mindful not to overload the air fryer basket with food, as this can prevent proper air circulation and cause uneven cooking.

4 Follow the recommended temperature and cooking times for the type of food you are cooking to ensure it is cooked thoroughly and safely.

5 Avoid using wet ingredients: To prevent smoking or malfunction, avoid using wet or moist ingredients in the air fryer.

6 Never leave the air fryer unattended while it is in use, and make sure to keep it out of reach of children and pets.

It's important to handle your air fryer with care, especially when attempting to remove a stuck piece of food. Avoid using excessive force to open the appliance, as this could damage the delicate internal components.

Frequently Asked Questions

1. Do I need to preheat the air fryer?

Most air fryers do require preheating before use, but the time and temperature can vary depending on the model and the food being cooked.

2. How do I know what temperature to set my air fryer to?

The temperature setting will depend on the food you are cooking. The air fryer typically comes with a manual that includes temperature and time guidelines for various foods.

3.Can I cook multiple items at once in an air fryer?

Yes, you can cook multiple items at once in an air fryer. However, you may need to adjust the cooking time and temperature accordingly.

4.Do I need to flip or shake the food in an air fryer during cooking?

It is recommended to flip or shake the food in the air fryer at least once during cooking to ensure even cooking and browning.

5. Can I cook raw meat in an air fryer?

- Yes, you can cook raw meat in an air fryer. It is recommended to follow the temperature and time guidelines for the specific type of meat you are cooking.

6. How do I store my air fryer when it's not in use?

- Store your air fryer in a cool, dry place when not in use, and avoid storing it in direct sunlight or areas with high humidity.

Conclusion

As the author of this recipe book about air fryers, I'm excited to share with you the endless possibilities that this incredible appliance has to offer. Whether you're a beginner or an experienced cook, an air fryer can bring a whole new level of excitement to your cooking routine.

The recipe book isn't just about the recipes themselves. It's also about exploring the full potential of your air fryer and learning new cooking techniques along the way. Whether you're looking to make healthier versions of your favorite comfort foods or you're ready to try something completely new, this recipe book is your go-to guide for all things air fryer. Enjoy the recipes and discover all the possibilities that an air fryer can offer.

Berry Muffins

Makes 8

Prep time: 15 minutes / Cook time: 12-17 minutes

Ingredients

- muffins
- 315 ml plus 1 tablespoon plain flour, divided
- 60 ml granulated sugar
- 2 tablespoons light brown sugar
- 2 teaspoons baking powder
- 2 eggs
- 160 ml whole milk
- 80 ml neutral oil
- 235 ml mixed fresh berries

Preparation instructions

1. In a medium bowl, stir together 315 ml of flour, the granulated sugar, brown sugar, and baking powder until mixed well.
2. In a small bowl, whisk the eggs, milk, and oil until combined. Stir the egg mixture into the dry Ingredients just until combined.
3. In another small bowl, toss the mixed berries with the remaining 1 tablespoon of flour until coated. Gently stir the berries into the batter.
4. Double up 16 foil muffin cups to make 8 cups.
5. Insert the crisper plate into the basket and the basket into the unit. Preheat the unit by selecting BAKE, setting the temperature to 156°C, and setting the time to 3 minutes. Select START/STOP to begin.
6. Once the unit is preheated, place 1 L into the basket and fill each three-quarters full with the batter.
7. Select BAKE, set the temperature to 156°C, and set the time for 17 minutes. Select START/STOP to begin.
8. After about 12 minutes, check the muffins. If they spring back when lightly touched with your finger, they are done. If not, resume cooking.
9. When the cooking is done, transfer the muffins to a wire rack to cool.
10. Repeat steps 6, 7, and 8 with the remaining muffin cups and batter.
11. Let the muffins cool for 10 minutes before serving.

Traditional English Breakfast

Serves 2

Prep time: 10 minutes / Cook time: 20 minutes

Ingredients

- 4 rashers of bacon
- 4 sausages
- 4 eggs
- 2 slices of black pudding
- 1 can of baked beans
- 2 tomatoes, halved
- 4 slices of bread, toasted
- Salt and pepper to taste

Preparation instructions

1. Preheat the air fryer to 200°C.
2. Place the bacon, sausages, black pudding, and tomato halves on a baking sheet.
3. Roast in the oven for 10-15 minutes, flipping

halfway through.

4. In a small saucepan, heat the baked beans over low heat.

5. Crack the eggs into a non-stick skillet and cook over medium heat until the whites are set and the yolks are still runny.

6. Season everything with salt and pepper to taste.

7. Serve the breakfast with the toasted bread, roasted tomatoes, beans, bacon, sausages, and eggs.

Traditional English Breakfast

Serves 4

Prep time: 10 minutes / Cook time: 15 minutes

Ingredients

- 4 hard-boiled eggs, peeled
- 1 lb ground pork sausage
- 1/2 cup all-purpose flour
- 2 eggs, beaten
- 1 cup panko breadcrumbs
- Salt and pepper to taste

Preparation instructions

1. Preheat the air fryer to 190°C.

2. Divide the sausage into 4 equal portions and flatten each portion into a patty.

3. Season the patties with salt and pepper.

4. Place an egg in the center of each patty and wrap the sausage around the egg, shaping it into a ball.

5. Coat each sausage ball in flour, shaking off any excess.

6. Dip each sausage ball into the beaten eggs, making sure it is coated all over.

7. Roll each sausage ball in the breadcrumbs,

pressing the breadcrumbs to adhere.

8. Place the sausage balls in the air fryer basket in a single layer.

9. Air fry for 15 minutes or until golden brown, flipping halfway through.

10. Serve the Scotch eggs warm with your favorite dipping sauce. Enjoy!

Star Anise Muffins

Serves 6 muffins

Prep time: 10 minutes / Cook time: 20 minutes

Ingredients

- 120g all-purpose flour
- 100g sugar
- 1 tsp baking powder
- 1/2 tsp baking soda
- 1/2 tsp ground star anise
- 120ml milk
- 60ml vegetable oil
- 1 egg
- 1 tsp vanilla extract

Preparation instructions

1. Preheat the air fryer to 320°F (160°C).

2. In a medium-sized mixing bowl, whisk together the flour, sugar, baking powder, baking soda, and ground star anise.

3. In a separate bowl, whisk together the milk, vegetable oil, egg, and vanilla extract.

4. Add the wet Ingredients to the dry Ingredients and mix until just combined.

5. Line a muffin tin with muffin cups and spoon the batter evenly into each cup.

6. Place the muffin tin in the air fryer basket and air fry for 20 minutes, or until the muffins are golden brown and a toothpick

inserted into the center comes out clean.

7. Remove the muffins from the air fryer and let cool for a few minutes before serving.

Breakfast Brownies

Serves 6 brownies

Prep time: 10 minutes / Cook time: 20 minutes

Ingredients

- 60g all-purpose flour
- 20g unsweetened cocoa powder
- 1/2 tsp baking powder
- 1/2 tsp baking soda
- 1/4 tsp salt
- 60g Greek yogurt
- 60ml maple syrup
- 60g unsweetened applesauce
- 1 egg
- 1 tsp vanilla extract

1/4 cup chocolate chips

Preparation instructions

1. Preheat the air fryer to 320°F (160°C).
2. In a medium-sized mixing bowl, whisk together the flour, cocoa powder, baking powder, baking soda, and salt.
3. In a separate bowl, whisk together the Greek yogurt, maple syrup, unsweetened applesauce, egg, and vanilla extract.
4. Add the wet Ingredients to the dry Ingredients and mix until just combined.
5. Fold in the chocolate chips.
6. Line a baking dish with parchment paper and pour the batter evenly into the dish.
7. Place the dish in the air fryer basket and air fry for 20 minutes, or until a toothpick inserted into the center comes out clean.
8. Remove the brownies from the air fryer and

let cool for a few minutes before slicing. Enjoy!

Breakfast Bars

Serves 6 bars

Prep time: 10 minutes / Cook time: 15 minutes

Ingredients

- 80g old-fashioned rolled oats
- 60g whole wheat flour
- 30g chopped almonds
- 40g raisins
- 1/4 tsp cinnamon
- 1/4 tsp salt
- 85g honey
- 60g unsweetened applesauce
- 1 egg
- 1 tsp vanilla extract

Preparation instructions

1. Preheat the air fryer to 320°F (160°C).
2. In a medium-sized mixing bowl, whisk together the oats, whole wheat flour, chopped almonds, raisins, cinnamon, and salt.
3. In a separate bowl, whisk together the honey, unsweetened applesauce, egg, and vanilla extract.
4. Add the wet Ingredients to the dry Ingredients and mix until well combined.
5. Line a baking dish with parchment paper and press the mixture evenly into the dish.
6. Place the dish in the air fryer basket and air fry for 15 minutes, or until the bars are golden brown.
7. Remove the bars from the air fryer and let cool for a few minutes before slicing. Serve it.

Breakfast Bars

Serves 2-4

Prep time: 5 minutes / Cook time: 15 minutes

Ingredients

- 1 large sweet potato
- 1 tbsp olive oil
- 1/4 tsp garlic powder
- Salt and pepper to taste

Preparation instructions

1. Preheat the air fryer to 190°C.
2. Peel and slice the sweet potato lengthwise into 1/4-inch thick slices.
3. In a small bowl, mix together the olive oil, garlic powder, salt, and pepper.
4. Brush the sweet potato slices with the oil mixture on both sides.
5. Place the sweet potato slices in the air fryer basket in a single layer.
6. Air fry for 15 minutes, flipping the slices halfway through, until they are tender and lightly browned.
7. Serve the sweet potato toast hot with your favorite toppings, such as avocado, eggs, or nut butter.

Air Fryer Breakfast Sausage Patties

Serves 2-4

Prep time: 5 minutes / Cook time: 10-12 minutes

Ingredients

- 450g ground breakfast sausage
- 1/4 tsp salt
- 1/4 tsp black pepper
- 1/4 tsp garlic powder
- 1/4 tsp onion powder

Preparation instructions

1. Preheat the air fryer to 190°C.
2. In a mixing bowl, combine the ground breakfast sausage with the salt, black pepper, garlic powder, and onion powder. Mix until well combined.
3. Form the sausage mixture into 2-3 inch patties.
4. Place the sausage patties in the air fryer basket in a single layer, making sure they are not touching.
5. Air fry for 10-12 minutes, flipping the patties halfway through, until they are browned and cooked through.
6. Remove the sausage patties from the air fryer and serve hot with your favorite breakfast sides.

Air Fryer Bubble and Squeak

Serves 2-4

Prep time: 5 minutes / Cook time: 10-12 minutes

Ingredients

- 450g potatoes, peeled and chopped
- 225g Brussels sprouts, trimmed and halved
- 50g butter
- 1/2 onion, chopped
- 1 garlic clove, minced
- Salt and pepper to taste
- 1 tablespoon olive oil

Preparation instructions

1. In a large pot of salted boiling water, cook the potatoes and Brussels sprouts until they are tender, about 15 minutes. Drain well and

set aside.

2. In a large skillet, melt the butter over medium heat. Add the chopped onion and garlic and cook until softened, about 5 minutes.

3. Add the cooked potatoes and Brussels sprouts to the skillet and use a potato masher to roughly mash the vegetables.

4. Season the mixture with salt and pepper to taste.

5. Use your hands to form the mixture into 6-8 patties, about 3 inches in diameter and 1 inch thick.

6. Brush the patties with olive oil on both sides.

7. Preheat the air fryer to 400°F (200°C).

8. Place the patties in the air fryer basket in a single layer, making sure they are not touching.

9. Air fry for 8-10 minutes, flipping the patties halfway through, until they are golden brown and crispy on both sides.

10. Serve the bubble and squeak hot with your favorite breakfast sides.

Herb Garlic Bread

Serves 4

Prep time: 10 minutes / Cook time: 5-7 minutes

Ingredients

- 1 small baguette, sliced into 1/2 inch thick rounds
- 3 tablespoons butter, softened
- 1 garlic clove, minced
- 1 tablespoon finely chopped fresh parsley
- 1 tablespoon finely chopped fresh basil
- Salt and pepper to taste

Preparation instructions

1. In a small bowl, combine the softened butter, minced garlic, chopped parsley, chopped basil, salt, and pepper. Mix until well combined.

2. Spread a generous amount of the herb butter mixture onto each slice of bread.

3. Preheat the air fryer to 370°F (187°C).

4. Arrange the slices of bread in the air fryer basket in a single layer, making sure they are not touching.

5. Air fry for 5-7 minutes, or until the bread is toasted and golden brown.

7. Remove the herb garlic bread from the air fryer and serve hot.

Easy Breakfast Wraps

Serves 4

Prep time: 10 minutes / Cook time: 8-10 minutes

Ingredients

- 4 large flour tortillas
- 4 eggs, beaten
- 4 slices of bacon, cooked and crumbled
- 56g shredded cheddar cheese
- 20g chopped green onions
- Salt and pepper to taste

Preparation instructions

1. Preheat the air fryer to 190°C.

2. Place a tortilla on a flat surface and add a quarter of the beaten eggs in the center of the tortilla.

3. Sprinkle a quarter of the crumbled bacon, shredded cheese, and chopped green onions on top of the eggs.

4. Season with salt and pepper to taste.

5. Roll up the tortilla tightly, tucking in the ends as you go.

6. Repeat the process with the remaining tortillas and filling.

7. Place the breakfast wraps in the air fryer basket, seam side down, in a single layer, making sure they are not touching.

8. Air fry for 8-10 minutes, or until the tortillas are crispy and golden brown.

9. Remove the breakfast wraps from the air fryer and let cool for a few minutes before slicing in half and serving.

Bacon and Egg Sandwich

Serves 2

Prep time: 5 minutes / Cook time: 10 minutes

Ingredients

- 4 slices of bread
- 4 slices of bacon
- 2 eggs
- 1 tablespoon butter
- Salt and pepper to taste

Preparation instructions

1. Preheat the air fryer to 190°C.

2. Cook the bacon in the air fryer for 6-8 minutes, until crispy. Remove and set aside.

3. Crack the eggs into a small bowl and whisk together with salt and pepper to taste.

4. Add the butter to a small oven-safe dish or ramekin and place in the air fryer for 1-2 minutes, until melted.

5. Pour the egg mixture into the melted butter and place back in the air fryer for 3-5 minutes, until the eggs are cooked to your liking.

6. Toast the bread in the air fryer for 1-2 minutes.

7. Assemble the sandwich by placing two slices

of bacon and a portion of the scrambled eggs on one slice of bread, then top with the other slice of bread.

8. Repeat with the remaining Ingredients to make the second sandwich.

9. Serve immediately.

Sausage and Tomato Sandwich

Serves 2

Prep time: 5 minutes / Cook time: 12 minutes

Ingredients

- 4 slices of bread
- 4 breakfast sausages
- 2 ripe tomatoes, sliced
- 1 tablespoon olive oil
- Salt and pepper to taste

Preparation instructions

1. Preheat the air fryer to 190°C.

2. Brush the sausages with olive oil and place them in the air fryer for 8-10 minutes, until cooked through and browned.

3. While the sausages are cooking, brush the tomato slices with olive oil and season with salt and pepper to taste.

4. Add the tomato slices to the air fryer basket and cook for 2-3 minutes, until slightly softened and browned.

5. Toast the bread in the air fryer for 1-2 minutes.

6. Assemble the sandwich by placing two cooked sausages and a few slices of tomato on one slice of bread, then top with the other slice of bread.

7. Repeat with the remaining Ingredients to make the second sandwich. Serve immediately.

Mini Blueberry Scones

Serves 8 mini scones

Prep time: 15 minutes / Cook time: 10minutes

Ingredients

- 125g all-purpose flour
- 50g granulated sugar
- 1 1/2 teaspoons baking powder
- 1/4 teaspoon salt
- 42g cold unsalted butter, cubed
- 40g fresh blueberries
- 60g heavy cream
- 1 large egg
- 1/2 teaspoon vanilla extract
1 tablespoon turbinado sugar

Preparation instructions

1. In a large mixing bowl, whisk together the flour, granulated sugar, baking powder, and salt.
2. Using a pastry cutter or your fingers, cut the cold butter into the flour mixture until it resembles coarse crumbs.
3. Gently fold in the blueberries, being careful not to break them.
4. In a separate mixing bowl, whisk together the heavy cream, egg, and vanilla extract.
5. Add the wet Ingredients to the dry Ingredients and stir until just combined.
6. Turn the dough out onto a lightly floured surface and knead gently a few times to bring it together.
7. Pat the dough into a circle about 1/2 inch thick and cut out 8 mini scones using a biscuit cutter or the rim of a small glass.
8. Sprinkle the tops of the scones with turbinado sugar.
9. Preheat the air fryer to 350°F (175°C). Place the scones in the air fryer basket in a single layer, leaving some space in between.
10. Air fry the scones for 8-10 minutes, until they are golden brown and cooked through. Serve warm with butter or jam.

Air Fryer Banana Bread

Serves 6

Prep time: 10minutes / Cook time: 30 minutes

Ingredients

- 2 ripe bananas, mashed
- 1/4 cup vegetable oil
- 1/2 cup granulated sugar
- 1 teaspoon vanilla extract
- 1 egg
- 1 cup all-purpose flour
- 1/2 teaspoon baking powder
- 1/2 teaspoon baking soda
- 1/2 teaspoon salt

Preparation instructions

1. In a mixing bowl, combine the mashed bananas, vegetable oil, sugar, vanilla extract, and egg.
2. In a separate mixing bowl, whisk together the flour, baking powder, baking soda, and salt.
3. Add the dry Ingredients to the wet Ingredients and stir until just combined.
4. Pour the batter into a greased loaf pan that will fit in your air fryer basket.
5. Preheat the air fryer to 320°F (160°C).
6. Place the loaf pan in the air fryer basket and air fry for 30 minutes or until a toothpick inserted in the center comes out clean.
7. Remove from the air fryer and let cool in the pan for 10 minutes before slicing and serving.

Air Fryer Breakfast Hash

Serves 2

Prep time: 10 minutes / Cook time: 20 minutes

Ingredients

- 2 medium potatoes, peeled and diced
- 1/2 small onion, diced
- 1/2 small bell pepper, diced
- 2 tablespoons vegetable oil
- 1/2 teaspoon salt
- 1/4 teaspoon black pepper
- 1/4 teaspoon garlic powder
- 2 large eggs

2 slices bacon, cooked and crumbled

Preparation instructions

1. Preheat the air fryer to 190°C.
2. In a large bowl, mix together the diced potatoes, onion, red pepper, green pepper, smoked paprika, garlic powder, salt, and pepper.
3. Transfer the mixture to the air fryer basket and cook for 15-20 minutes, shaking the basket occasionally to ensure even cooking.
4. Create four wells in the hash mixture and crack an egg into each well.
5. Cook for an additional 5-7 minutes or until the egg whites are set and the yolks are cooked to your desired level of doneness.
6. Serve hot and enjoy!

Air Fryer French Toast Sticks

Serves 4

Prep time: 10 minutes / Cook time: 8 minutes

Ingredients

- 6 slices of bread, cut into sticks
- 2 eggs
- 1/2 cup milk
- 1 tablespoon vanilla extract
- 1 teaspoon cinnamon
- 1/4 teaspoon nutmeg
- Maple syrup and powdered sugar, for serving

Preparation instructions

1. Preheat the air fryer to 370°F (187°C).
2. In a shallow bowl, whisk together the eggs, milk, vanilla extract, cinnamon, and nutmeg.
3. Dip each bread stick into the egg mixture, making sure to coat each side well.
4. Place the bread sticks in a single layer in the air fryer basket.
5. Cook for 4 minutes, flip the sticks over, and cook for an additional 4 minutes.
6. Serve hot with maple syrup and powdered sugar on top.

Cheesy Bell Pepper Eggs

Serves 4

Prep time: 10 minutes / Cook time: 15 minutes

Ingredients

- 4 medium green peppers
- 85 g cooked ham, chopped
- ¼ medium onion, peeled and chopped
- 8 large eggs
- 235 ml mild Cheddar cheese

Preparation instructions

1. Cut the tops off each pepper. Remove the seeds and the white membranes with a small knife. Place ham and onion into each pepper.
2. Crack 2 eggs into each pepper. Top with 60 ml cheese per pepper. Place into the air fryer basket.
3. Adjust the temperature to 200°C and air fry

for 15 minutes.

4. When fully cooked, peppers will be tender and eggs will be firm. Serve immediately

Puffed Egg Tarts

Makes 4 tarts

Prep time: 10 minutes / Cook time: 42 minutes

Ingredients

- Oil, for spraying
- Plain flour, for dusting
- 1 (340 g) sheet frozen puff pastry, thawed
- 180 ml shredded Cheddar cheese, divided
- 4 large eggs
- 2 teaspoons chopped fresh parsley
- Salt and freshly ground black pepper, to
- taste

Preparation instructions :

1. Preheat the air fryer to 200ºC.
2. Line the air fryer basket with parchment and spray lightly with oil.
3. Lightly dust your work surface with flour. Unfold the puff pastry and cut it into 4 equal squares.
4. Place 2 squares in the prepared basket. Cook for 10 minutes. Remove the basket.
5. Press the centre of each tart shell with a spoon to make an indentation. Sprinkle 3 tablespoons of cheese into each indentation and crack 1 egg into the centre of each tart shell. Cook for another 7 to 11 minutes, or until the eggs are cooked to your desired doneness.
6. Repeat with the remaining puff pastry squares, cheese, and eggs. Sprinkle evenly with the parsley, and season with salt and black pepper.

7. Serve immediately.

Air Fryer Avocado Toast

Serves 2

Prep time: 5 minutes / Cook time: 5 minutes

Ingredients

- 2 slices of bread
- 1 ripe avocado
- 1/4 teaspoon garlic powder
- Salt and pepper, to taste
- 2 eggs
- 1 tablespoon olive oil
- Red pepper flakes, for serving (optional)

Preparation instructions :

1. Preheat the air fryer to 190°C.
2. Mash the ripe avocado in a small bowl and mix in the garlic powder, salt, and pepper.
3. Brush each slice of bread with olive oil on both sides and place them in the air fryer basket.
4. Cook for 3 minutes, flip the bread slices over, and cook for an additional 2 minutes or until they are toasted to your desired level of crispiness.
5. While the bread is toasting, crack an egg into each of the avocado halves and place them in the air fryer basket.
6. Cook for 5 minutes or until the egg whites are set and the yolks are cooked to your desired level of doneness.
7. Spread the mashed avocado on top of each toast slice and place an egg-filled avocado half on top of each.
8. Sprinkle with red pepper flakes, if desired, and serve hot.

Air Fried Breakfast Casserole

Serves 4

Prep time: 10 minutes / Cook time: 10-15 minutes

Ingredients

- 6 large eggs
- 120 ml of milk
- 1/2 teaspoon of salt
- 1/4 teaspoon of black pepper
- 1/4 teaspoon of paprika
- 1/4 teaspoon of garlic powder
- 1/4 teaspoon of onion powder
- 30g of shredded cheddar cheese
- 30g of chopped ham
- 30g of chopped bell pepper
- 30g of chopped onion

Preparation instructions

1. In a large bowl, whisk together the eggs, milk, salt, black pepper, paprika, garlic powder, and onion powder.
2. Stir in the shredded cheddar cheese, chopped ham, bell pepper, and onion.
3. Pour the egg mixture into a greased 7-inch baking dish that will fit into your air fryer basket.
4. Preheat the air fryer to 180°C.
5. Place the baking dish in the air fryer basket and cook for 10-15 minutes, or until the eggs are set and the cheese is melted and bubbly.
6. Use a spatula to remove the casserole from the baking dish and serve.

Air Fried Kedgeree

Serves 4

Prep time: 10 minutes / Cook time: 25-30 minutes

Ingredients

- 200g basmati rice
- 500ml water
- 2 eggs
- 2 tablespoons (30ml) vegetable oil
- 1 onion, finely chopped
- 1 clove of garlic, minced
- 1 teaspoon ground cumin
- 1 teaspoon ground coriander
- 1/2 teaspoon ground turmeric
- 1/2 teaspoon paprika
- 1/2 teaspoon salt
- 1/4 teaspoon black pepper
- 300g smoked haddock fillet, skin removed and flaked
- 15g chopped fresh parsley
- 1 lemon, cut into wedges

Preparation instructions

1. Rinse the rice under cold water and drain. In a medium-sized saucepan, combine the rice and water. Bring to a boil over high heat, then reduce the heat to low and cover with a lid. Simmer for 12-15 minutes or until the water is absorbed and the rice is cooked.
2. In a small bowl, beat the eggs and set aside.
3. In a large frying pan, heat the vegetable oil over medium heat. Add the chopped onion and garlic and sauté for 2-3 minutes until soft.
4. Add the ground cumin, coriander, turmeric, paprika, salt, and black pepper to the frying pan and stir to combine.
5. Add the flaked smoked haddock to the frying pan and cook for 2-3 minutes until heated

through.

6. Add the cooked rice to the frying pan and stir to combine with the haddock and spices.

7. Pour the beaten eggs into the frying pan and stir gently until the eggs are cooked and scrambled.

8. Transfer the kedgeree to the air fryer basket and cook for 5-7 minutes at 180°C or until heated through and lightly crispy.

9. Sprinkle with chopped fresh parsley and serve with lemon wedges.

Air Fried Breakfast Bruschetta

Serves 4

Prep time: 10 minutes / Cook time: 10 minutes

Ingredients

- 4 slices of bread, cut into 1 cm thick slices
- 2 tablespoons (30ml) olive oil
- 4 slices of bacon
- 4 cherry tomatoes, quartered
- 4 eggs
- 1/4 cup (15g) grated Parmesan cheese
- Salt and black pepper, to taste
- Fresh basil leaves, chopped (optional)

Preparation instructions

1. Preheat the air fryer to 180°C.

2. Brush both sides of the bread slices with olive oil.

3. Place the bread slices in a single layer in the air fryer basket.

4. Air fry for 4-5 minutes until the bread is crispy and lightly golden.

5. Meanwhile, cook the bacon in a frying pan over medium heat until crispy. Remove from the pan and set aside.

6. In the same frying pan, add the cherry

tomatoes and cook for 2-3 minutes until softened.

7. Crack the eggs into the frying pan with the cherry tomatoes and cook to your liking.

8. Once the bread is done, remove from the air fryer basket and place on a serving plate.

9. Top each bread slice with a slice of bacon, cherry tomatoes, and a cooked egg.

10. Sprinkle grated Parmesan cheese on top and season with salt and black pepper. Garnish with chopped fresh basil leaves (optional).

11. Serve immediately.

Air Fried Welsh Rarebit

Serves 4

Prep time: 10 minutes / Cook time: 10 minutes

Ingredients

- 4 slices of bread, cut into 1 cm thick slices
- 25g butter
- 25g plain flour
- 100ml milk
- 100g grated Cheddar cheese
- 1 teaspoon (5g) Dijon mustard
- 1 teaspoon (5g) Worcestershire sauce
- Salt and black pepper, to taste

Preparation instructions

1. Preheat the air fryer to 180°C.

2. Melt the butter in a saucepan over medium heat.

3. Add the flour and whisk until smooth. Cook for 1-2 minutes until the mixture turns golden brown.

4. Gradually whisk in the milk, making sure there are no lumps.

5. Keep stirring until the mixture thickens, then remove from heat.

6. Add the grated Cheddar cheese, mustard, Worcestershire sauce, salt, and black pepper. Stir until the cheese is melted and the mixture is well combined.

7. Place the bread slices in a single layer in the air fryer basket.

8. Spoon the cheese mixture on top of each bread slice, spreading it evenly.

9. Air fry for 4-5 minutes until the cheese is melted and bubbly.Serve immediately.

Air-fried breakfast sandwich with sausage, egg, and cheese

Serves 2

Prep time: 5 minutes / Cook time:15 minutes

Ingredients

- 2 English muffins, split in half
- 2 breakfast sausages
- 2 slices of Cheddar cheese
- 2 large eggs
- Salt and pepper, to taste
- Cooking spray

Preparation instructions

1. Preheat the air fryer to 180°C.

2. Lightly coat the air fryer basket with cooking spray.

3. Place the breakfast sausages in the air fryer basket and cook for 5-7 minutes until browned and cooked through.

4. Remove the sausages from the basket and set aside.

5. Crack the eggs into a bowl, season with salt and pepper, and whisk until well beaten.

6. Pour the eggs into the air fryer basket and cook for 4-5 minutes until set.

7. Place the English muffins, cut side up, in the air fryer basket and cook for 2-3 minutes until lightly toasted.

8. Top each English muffin half with a sausage, a slice of Cheddar cheese, and a cooked egg.

9. Place the assembled sandwiches in the air fryer basket and cook for 2-3 minutes until the cheese is melted. Serve immediately.

Air Fryer Crispy Chicken Tenders

Serves 4

Prep time: 10 minutes / Cook time: 10-12 minutes

Ingredients

- 450 g chicken tenders
- 100 g panko breadcrumbs
- 1 tsp. paprika
- 1 tsp. garlic powder
- 1 tsp. salt
- 1/2 tsp. black pepper
- 2 eggs, beaten

Preparation instructions

1. Preheat air fryer to 200°C.
2. In a shallow dish, mix together breadcrumbs, paprika, garlic powder, salt, and pepper.
3. Dip chicken tenders in beaten eggs, then coat in breadcrumb mixture.
4. Place chicken tenders in air fryer basket in a single layer, making sure they are not touching.
5. Cook for 10-12 minutes, flipping halfway through, until chicken is cooked through and golden brown.

Air Fryer Buffalo Chicken Wings

Serves 4

Prep time: 10 minutes / Cook time: 25-30 minutes /

Ingredients

- 900 g chicken wings
- 60 ml hot sauce
- 60 ml melted butter
- 1 tsp. garlic powder
- 1 tsp. salt
- 1/2 tsp. black pepper

Preparation instructions

1. Preheat air fryer to 190°C.
2. Pat chicken wings dry with paper towels.
3. In a large bowl, whisk together hot sauce, melted butter, garlic powder, salt, and black pepper.
4. Toss chicken wings in sauce mixture until evenly coated.
5. Place chicken wings in air fryer basket in a single layer, making sure they are not touching.
6. Cook for 25-30 minutes, flipping halfway through, until chicken is cooked through and crispy.

Chicken Satay Salad

Serves 4

Prep time: 20 minutes / Cook time: 15 minutes

Ingredients

- For the chicken satay:
- 500 g boneless, skinless chicken breasts, cut into bite-sized pieces
- 1/2 cup coconut milk
- 2 tbsp soy sauce
- 2 tbsp brown sugar
- 1 tbsp curry powder
- 1 tsp ground cumin
- 1 tsp ground coriander
- 1 garlic clove, minced

- 1 tbsp lime juice
- Salt and pepper
- Skewers, soaked in water for 30 minutes
- For the salad:
- 120g mixed greens
- 1 red pepper, sliced
- 1/2 red onion, sliced
- 30gchopped peanuts
- 2 tbsp chopped fresh cilantro
- For the dressing:
- 60 g peanut butter
- 30 ml soy sauce
- 30 ml rice vinegar
- 15 ml honey
- 15 ml sesame oil
- 1 garlic clove, minced
- 2-3 tbsp water, as needed to thin out the dressing

Preparation instructions

1. In a medium bowl, whisk together the coconut milk, soy sauce, brown sugar, curry powder, cumin, coriander, garlic, lime juice, salt, and pepper. Add the chicken pieces and toss to coat. Marinate for at least 1 hour, or overnight in the fridge.

2. Preheat a grill or grill pan to medium-high heat. Thread the chicken pieces onto the soaked skewers.

3. Grill the chicken skewers for about 10-12 minutes, turning occasionally, until cooked through and slightly charred.

4. In a large bowl, combine the mixed greens, sliced red pepper, and red onion.

5. In a small bowl, whisk together the peanut butter, soy sauce, rice vinegar, honey, sesame oil, garlic, and water until smooth.

6. To assemble the salad, divide the greens

mixture among 4 plates. Top each plate with the grilled chicken skewers, chopped peanuts, and fresh cilantro. Drizzle with the peanut dressing and serve.

Air Fryer Turkey Meatballs with Zucchini Noodles

Serves 4

Prep time: 15 minutes / Cook time: 20 minutes

Ingredients

For the meatballs:
- 500 g ground turkey
- 50 g breadcrumbs
- 1 egg, lightly beaten
- 25 g grated Parmesan cheese
- 2 garlic cloves, minced
- 1 tsp dried oregano
- 1 tsp dried basil
- Salt and pepper
- For the zucchini noodles:
- 4 medium zucchini, spiralized
- 2 tbsp olive oil
- 2 garlic cloves, minced
- Salt and pepper

Preparation instructions

1. Preheat your air fryer to 190°C.

2. In a large mixing bowl, combine the ground turkey, breadcrumbs, Parmesan cheese, egg, garlic powder, onion powder, dried basil, dried oregano, salt, and pepper. Mix well until everything is evenly combined.

3. Use your hands to shape the mixture into 1-inch meatballs.

4. Place the meatballs in the air fryer basket, making sure to leave enough space between each meatball.

5. Air fry the meatballs for 12-15 minutes, or until they are golden brown and cooked through.
6. While the meatballs are cooking, prepare the zucchini noodles. Cut the zucchini into thin, noodle-like strips using a vegetable peeler or spiralizer.
7. Heat the olive oil in a large skillet over medium-high heat. Add the zucchini noodles and cook for 2-3 minutes, or until they are tender and lightly browned.
8. Season the zucchini noodles with salt and pepper to taste.
9. Serve the turkey meatballs with the zucchini noodles on the side. Enjoy!

Air Fryer Chicken Breast with Garlic and Herbs

Serves 2

Prep time: 5 minutes / Cook time: 15 minutes

Ingredients
- 2 boneless, skinless chicken breasts
- 2 tbsp olive oil
- 1 tsp garlic powder
- 1 tsp dried thyme
- Salt and pepper to taste

Preparation instructions
1. Preheat the air fryer to 190°C.
2. Brush the chicken breasts with olive oil and season with garlic powder, dried thyme, salt, and pepper.
3. Place the chicken breasts in the air fryer basket and cook for 15 minutes, flipping halfway through, until the internal temperature reaches 75°C.

Air Fryer Chicken Tikka

Serves 4

Prep time: 20 minutes / Cook time: 20 minutes

Ingredients
- 4 boneless, skinless chicken breasts (600g), cut into bite-sized pieces
- 1 cup plain Greek yogurt (240ml)
- 2 tbsp vegetable oil (30ml)
- 2 tbsp garam masala (10g)
- 2 tsp ground cumin (4g)
- 1 tsp smoked paprika (2g)
- 1 tsp ground ginger (2g)
- 1/2 tsp garlic powder (1g)
- 1/2 tsp salt
- 1/4 tsp black pepper
- Cooking spray

Preparation instructions
1. In a bowl, whisk together the Greek yogurt, vegetable oil, garam masala, cumin, paprika, ginger, garlic powder, salt, and pepper until well combined.
2. Add the chicken pieces to the bowl and toss to coat evenly with the marinade.
3. Cover the bowl with plastic wrap and refrigerate for at least 1 hour, or up to overnight.
4. Preheat the air fryer to 200°C.
5. Remove the chicken from the marinade and shake off any excess.
6. Place the chicken pieces in the air fryer basket and spray with cooking spray.
7. Cook for 10-12 minutes, flipping halfway through, until the chicken is cooked through and golden brown.
8. Serve the chicken tikka with rice, naan bread, and your choice of chutney or raita.

Air Fryer Turkey Burgers

Serves 4

Prep time: 10 minutes / Cook time: 10 minutes

Ingredients

- 500g ground turkey
- 1/2 onion, finely chopped
- 2 garlic cloves, minced
- 1 tsp dried thyme
- 1 tsp salt
- 1/2 tsp black pepper
- 4 burger buns
- Lettuce, tomato, and condiments, for serving

Preparation instructions

1. Preheat the air fryer to 200°C.
2. In a large bowl, mix together the ground turkey, onion, garlic, thyme, salt, and pepper until well combined.
3. Form the mixture into 4 patties and place them in the air fryer basket.
4. Cook the turkey burgers for 10 minutes, flipping halfway through, until cooked through.
5. Toast the burger buns in the air fryer for 1-2 minutes.
6. Assemble the burgers with lettuce, tomato, and your favorite condiments.

Air Fryer Chicken Parmesan

Serves 4

Prep time: 15 minutes / Cook time: 15 minutes

Ingredients

- 4 boneless, skinless chicken breasts (600g)
- 120g Italian-seasoned breadcrumbs
- 50g grated Parmesan cheese
- 1 tsp garlic powder
- 1 tsp paprika
- Salt and pepper
- 1 egg, beaten
- Cooking spray
- 240ml marinara sauce
- 120g shredded mozzarella cheese

Preparation instructions

1. Preheat the air fryer to 200°C.
2. In a shallow bowl, mix together the breadcrumbs, Parmesan cheese, garlic powder, paprika, salt, and pepper.
3. In a separate bowl, beat the egg.
4. Dip each chicken breast in the egg mixture, then dredge in the breadcrumb mixture, pressing the breadcrumbs onto the chicken to coat well.
5. Place the chicken breasts in the air fryer basket and spray with cooking spray.
6. Cook for 12 minutes, flipping halfway through, until the chicken is cooked through and the breadcrumbs are crispy.
7. Spoon marinara sauce over each chicken breast, then sprinkle with mozzarella cheese.
8. Return the chicken to the air fryer and cook for an additional 2-3 minutes, until the cheese is melted and bubbly.
9. Serve the chicken parmesan with your choice of pasta or a side salad.

Turkey Satay Salad

Serves 4

Prep time: 20 minutes / Cook time: 15 minutes

Ingredients

- 4 turkey breasts (600g), cut into bite-sized pieces

- 120g natural peanut butter
- 2 tbsp soy sauce
- 2 tbsp honey
- 1 tbsp lime juice
- 1/2 tsp garlic powder
- 1/4 tsp ground ginger (0. 5g)
- 1/4 tsp salt
- 1/4 tsp black pepper
- 200g mixed salad greens
- 1 red bell pepper , sliced
- 1 yellow bell pepper , sliced
- 70g roasted peanuts , chopped
- Cooking spray

Preparation instructions

1. In a bowl, whisk together the peanut butter, soy sauce, honey, lime juice, garlic powder, ginger, salt, and pepper until well combined.
2. Add the turkey pieces to the bowl and toss to coat evenly with the marinade.
3. Cover the bowl with plastic wrap and refrigerate for at least 1 hour, or up to overnight.
4. Preheat the air fryer to 200°C.
5. Remove the turkey from the marinade and shake off any excess.
6. Spray the air fryer basket with cooking spray.
7. Add the turkey pieces to the basket and cook for 10-12 minutes, flipping halfway through, until the turkey is cooked through and golden brown.
8. In a large bowl, toss together the mixed salad greens, sliced bell peppers, and chopped peanuts.
9. Divide the salad mixture among four plates. Top each salad with the cooked turkey pieces.
10. Drizzle any remaining peanut sauce over the salads and serve immediately.

Chicken Kievs

Serves 4

Prep time: 20 minutes / Cook time: 25 minutes

Ingredients

- 6 (150-175g each) chicken breasts, skinless and boneless
- 1 tbsp olive oil
- 1 tsp hot paprika
- Sea salt and ground black pepper, to taste
- 80g dried breadcrumbs
- 80g parmesan, grated

Preparation instructions

1. Rub the chicken with olive oil, paprika, salt, and black pepper. Then, roll the chicken over the breadcrumbs.
2. Insert crisper plates in both drawers. Spray the crisper plates with nonstick cooking oil.
3. Place the chicken breasts in the basket and spray the tops lightly with cooking spray.
4. Preheat the air fryer to 190°C
5. Cook for 20-25 minutes, until the chicken is cooked through and the breadcrumbs are golden brown and crispy.
6. At the halfway point, flip the chicken breasts with silicone-tipped tongs and top them with parmesan cheese. Reinsert drawers to resume cooking.
7. Enjoy!

Herb Chicken with Asparagus

Serves 4

Prep time: 10 minutes / Cook time: 20 minutes

Ingredients

- 4 boneless, skinless chicken breasts (600g)
- 300g asparagus, trimmed
- 2 tbsp olive oil
- 1 tbsp fresh thyme leaves
- 1 tbsp fresh rosemary leaves
- 1 tbsp fresh parsley leaves, chopped
- 1 lemon, juiced
- Salt and black pepper

Preparation instructions

1. Preheat the air fryer to 200°C.
2. In a small bowl, whisk together the olive oil, thyme leaves, rosemary leaves, parsley leaves, and lemon juice.
3. Season the chicken breasts with a little salt and black pepper, then brush them all over with the herb and lemon mixture.
4. Place the chicken breasts in the air fryer basket and cook for 10 minutes.
5. After 10 minutes, add the trimmed asparagus to the basket, then cook for a further 10 minutes.
6. Check that the chicken is cooked through and the asparagus is tender before serving hot.

Mini Meatloaf Cups

Serves 4

Prep time: 15minutes / Cook time: 25 minutes

Ingredients

- 500g lean ground turkey
- 60g breadcrumbs (60g)
- 30g grated Parmesan cheese
- 60ml milk
- 1 egg, beaten
- 1 small onion, finely chopped
- 1 clove garlic, minced
- 1 tsp dried oregano
- 1 tsp dried basil
- 1 tsp salt
- 1/4 tsp black pepper
- Cooking spray

Preparation instructions

1. Preheat the air fryer to 180°C.
2. In a large bowl, mix together the ground turkey, breadcrumbs, Parmesan cheese, milk, beaten egg, chopped onion, minced garlic, dried oregano, dried basil, salt, and black pepper until well combined.
3. Grease a 12-cup muffin tin with cooking spray.
4. Divide the meat mixture evenly among the 12 muffin cups, pressing it down firmly.
5. Place the muffin tin in the air fryer basket and cook for 20-25 minutes, until the meatloaf cups are cooked through and browned on top.
6. Serve hot, garnished with chopped fresh herbs or your choice of sauce.

Lemon Chicken with Garlic

Serves 4

Prep time: 5minutes / Cook time: 20-25 minutes

Ingredients

- 8 bone-in chicken thighs, skin on
- 1 tablespoon olive oil
- 1½ teaspoons lemon-pepper seasoning
- ½ teaspoon paprika
- ½ teaspoon garlic powder
- ¼ teaspoon freshly ground black pepper

- Juice of ½ lemon

Preparation instructions

1. Preheat the air fryer to 180°C.
2. Place the chicken in a large bowl and drizzle with the olive oil. Top with the lemon-pepper seasoning, paprika, garlic powder, and freshly ground black pepper. Toss until thoroughly coated.
3. Working in batches if necessary, arrange the chicken in a single layer in the basket of the air fryer. Pausing halfway through the cooking time to turn the chicken, air fry for 20 to 25 minutes, until a thermometer inserted into the thickest piece registers 76°C.
4. Transfer the chicken to a serving platter and squeeze the lemon juice over the top.

Golden Chicken Cutlets

Serves 4

Prep time: 15minutes / Cook time: 15 minutes

Ingredients

- 2 tablespoons panko breadcrumbs
- 20 g grated Parmesan cheese
- ⅛ tablespoon paprika
- ½ tablespoon garlic powder
- 2 large eggs
- 4 chicken cutlets
- 1 tablespoon parsley
- Salt and ground black pepper, to taste
- Cooking spray

Preparation instructions

1. Preheat air fryer to 200°C. Spritz the air fryer basket with cooking spray.
2. Combine the breadcrumbs, Parmesan, paprika, garlic powder, salt, and ground black pepper in a large bowl. Stir to mix well. Beat the eggs in a separate bowl.
3. Dredge the chicken cutlets in the beaten eggs, then roll over the breadcrumbs mixture to coat well. Shake the excess off.
4. Transfer the chicken cutlets in the preheated air fryer and spritz with cooking spray.
5. Air fry for 15 minutes or until crispy and golden brown. Flip the cutlets halfway through.
6. Serve with parsley on top.

Mediterranean Stuffed Chicken Breasts

Serves 4

Prep time: 5minutes / Cook time: 20-25minutes

Ingredients

- 4 small boneless, skinless chicken breast halves (about 680 g)
- Salt and freshly ground black pepper, to taste
- 115 g goat cheese
- 6 pitted Kalamata olives, coarsely chopped
- Zest of ½ lemon
- 1 teaspoon minced fresh rosemary or ½ teaspoon ground dried rosemary
- 50 g almond meal
- 60 ml balsamic vinegar
- 6 tablespoons unsalted butter

Preparation instructions

1. Preheat the air fryer to 180°C.
2. With a boning knife, cut a wide pocket into the thickest part of each chicken breast half, taking care not to cut all the way through. Season the chicken evenly on both sides

with salt and freshly ground black pepper.

3. In a small bowl, mix the cheese, olives, lemon zest, and rosemary. Stuff the pockets with the cheese mixture and secure with toothpicks.

4. Place the almond meal in a shallow bowl and dredge the chicken, shaking off the excess. Coat lightly with olive oil spray.

5 Working in batches if necessary, arrange the chicken breasts in a single layer in the air fryer basket. Pausing halfway through the cooking time to flip the chicken, air fry for 20 to 25 minutes, until a thermometer inserted into the thickest part registers 76°C.

6. While the chicken is baking, prepare the sauce. In a small pan over medium heat, simmer the balsamic vinegar until thick and syrupy, about 5 minutes. Set aside until the chicken is done. When ready to serve, warm the sauce over medium heat and whisk in the butter, 1 tablespoon at a time, until melted and smooth. Season to taste with salt and pepper.

7. Serve the chicken breasts with the sauce drizzled on top.

Breaded Turkey Cutlets

Serves 4

Prep time: 5 minutes / Cook time: 8 minutes

Ingredients

- 60 g whole wheat bread crumbs
- ¼ teaspoon paprika
- ¼ teaspoon salt
- ¼ teaspoon black pepper
- ⅛ teaspoon dried sage
- ⅛ teaspoon garlic powder
- 1 egg
- 4 turkey breast cutlets
- Chopped fresh parsley, for serving

Preparation instructions

1. Preheat the air fryer to 192°C.

2. In a medium shallow bowl, whisk together the bread crumbs, paprika, salt, black pepper, sage, and garlic powder.

3. In a separate medium shallow bowl, whisk the egg until frothy.

4. Dip each turkey cutlet into the egg mixture, then into the bread crumb mixture, coating the outside with the crumbs. Place the breaded turkey cutlets in a single layer in the bottom of the air fryer basket, making sure that they don't touch each other.

5. Bake for 4 minutes. Turn the cutlets over, then bake for 4 minutes more, or until the internal temperature reaches 76°C. Sprinkle on the parsley and serve.

Stuffed Turkey Roulade

Serves 4

Prep time: 10 minutes / Cook time: 45 minutes

Ingredients

- 1 (900 g) boneless turkey breast, skin removed
- 1 teaspoon salt
- ½ teaspoon black pepper
- 115 g goat cheese
- 1 tablespoon fresh thyme
- 1 tablespoon fresh sage
- 2 garlic cloves, minced
- 2 tablespoons olive oil
- Fresh chopped parsley, for garnish

Preparation instructions

1. Preheat the air fryer to 192°C.
2. Using a sharp knife, butterfly the turkey breast, and season both sides with salt and pepper and set aside.
3. In a small bowl, mix together the goat cheese, thyme, sage, and garlic.
4. Spread the cheese mixture over the turkey breast, then roll it up tightly, tucking the ends underneath.
5. Place the turkey breast roulade onto a piece of aluminum foil, wrap it up, and place it into the air fryer.
6. Bake for 30 minutes. Remove the foil from the turkey breast and brush the top with oil, then continue cooking for another 10 to 15 minutes, or until the outside has browned and the internal temperature reaches 76°C.
7. Remove and cut into 1-inch-wide slices and serve with a sprinkle of parsley on top.

Easy Chicken Nachos

Serves 8

Prep time: 5minutes / Cook time: 5 minutes

Ingredients

- Oil, for spraying
- 420 g shredded cooked chicken
- 1 (30 g) package ranch seasoning
- 60 g sour cream
- 55 g corn tortilla chips
- 75 g bacon bits
- 235 g shredded Cheddar cheese
- 1 tablespoon chopped spring onions

Preparation instructions

1. Line the air fryer basket with parchment and spray lightly with oil.

2. In a small bowl, mix together the chicken, ranch seasoning, and sour cream.
3. Place the tortilla chips in the prepared basket and top with the chicken mixture. Add the bacon bits, Cheddar cheese, and spring onions.
4. Air fry at 220°C for 3 to 5 minutes, or until heated through and the cheese is melted.

Air Fried Chicken Wings with Buffalo Sauce

Serves 6

Prep time: 10minutes / Cook time: 20 minutes

Ingredients

- 16 chicken drumettes (party wings)
- Chicken seasoning or rub, to taste
- 1 teaspoon garlic powder
- Ground black pepper, to taste
- 60 ml buffalo wings sauce
- Cooking spray

Preparation instructions

1. Preheat the air fryer to 200°C. Spritz the air fryer basket with cooking spray.
2. Rub the chicken wings with chicken seasoning, garlic powder, and ground black pepper on a clean work surface.
3. Arrange the chicken wings in the preheated air fryer. Spritz with cooking spray. Air fry for 10 minutes or until lightly browned. Shake the basket halfway through.
4. Transfer the chicken wings in a large bowl, then pour in the buffalo wings sauce and toss to coat well.
5. Put the wings back to the air fryer and cook for an additional 7 minutes.
6. Serve immediately.

Firecracker Prawns

Serves 4

Prep time: 10 minutes / Cook time: 10 minutes

Ingredients

- 16 chicken drumettes (party wings)
- 500g raw prawns, peeled and deveined
- 2 tbsp cornstarch
- 1 tbsp sesame oil
- 1 tbsp soy sauce
- 1 tbsp honey
- 1 tbsp sriracha sauce
- 2 cloves garlic, minced
- 1/2 inch ginger, peeled and grated
- 1 green onion, thinly sliced

Preparation instructions

1. Preheat the air fryer to 200°C.
2. In a small bowl, whisk together the cornstarch, sesame oil, soy sauce, honey, sriracha sauce, minced garlic, and grated ginger until well combined.
3. Add the prawns to the bowl and toss to coat evenly with the sauce.
4. Place the prawns in the air fryer basket in a single layer and cook for 5 minutes.
5. After 5 minutes, flip the prawns over and cook for a further 5 minutes until they are pink and cooked through.
6. Serve hot, garnished with sliced green onions.

Firecracker Prawns

Serves 4

Prep time: 10 minutes / Cook time: 8 minutes

Ingredients

- 500g raw prawns, peeled and deveined
- 2 tbsp olive oil
- 2 tbsp lemon juice
- 1 tbsp lemon zest
- 1 tbsp black pepper
- 2 cloves garlic, minced
- Salt

Preparation instructions

1. Preheat the air fryer to 200°C.
2. In a small bowl, whisk together the olive oil, lemon juice, lemon zest, black pepper, minced garlic, and a pinch of salt.
3. Add the prawns to the bowl and toss to coat evenly with the mixture.
4. Place the prawns in the air fryer basket in a single layer and cook for 4 minutes.
5. After 4 minutes, flip the prawns over and cook for a further 4 minutes until they are pink and cooked through.
6. Serve hot with your choice of sides.

Baked Grouper with Tomatoes and Garlic

Serves 4

Prep time: 5 minutes / Cook time: 12 minutes

Ingredients

- 4 grouper fillets
- ½ teaspoon salt
- 3 garlic cloves, minced
- 1 tomato, sliced
- 45 g sliced Kalamata olives
- 10 g fresh dill, roughly chopped
- Juice of 1 lemon
- ¼ cup olive oil

Preparation instructions

1. Preheat the air fryer to 192°C.
2. Season the grouper fillets on all sides with salt, then place into the air fryer basket and top with the minced garlic, tomato slices, olives, and fresh dill.
3. Drizzle the lemon juice and olive oil over the top of the grouper, then bake for 10 to 12 minutes, or until the internal temperature reaches 64°C.

Air Fryer Fish and Chips

Serves 2

Prep time: 15 minutes / Cook time: 20 minutes

Ingredients

- 2 cod fillets (300g)
- 100g plain flour
- 1 tsp paprika
- 1 tsp garlic powder
- 1 tsp onion powder
- Salt and pepper
- 1 egg, beaten
- 100g breadcrumbs
- Cooking spray

Preparation instructions

1. Preheat the air fryer to 200°C.
2. In a shallow dish, mix together the flour, paprika, garlic powder, onion powder, salt, and pepper.
3. Dip each cod fillet in the flour mixture, then the beaten egg, and finally the breadcrumbs.
4. Place the breaded cod fillets in the air fryer basket and spray with cooking spray.
5. Cook for 10 minutes, then flip the fillets over and cook for a further 10 minutes until golden and crispy.
6. Serve with chips and tartar sauce.

Lemon Garlic Air Fryer Scallops

Serves 4

Prep time: 10 minutes / Cook time: 6 minutes

Ingredients

- 500g scallops
- 2 tbsp olive oil (30ml)
- 2 cloves garlic, minced
- 2 tbsp lemon juice (30ml)
- 1 tsp lemon zest
- Salt and pepper
- Chopped parsley for garnish

Preparation instructions

1. Preheat the air fryer to 200°C.
2. In a bowl, mix together the olive oil, minced garlic, lemon juice, lemon zest, salt, and pepper.
3. Add the scallops to the bowl and toss to coat evenly with the mixture.

4. Place the scallops in the air fryer basket in a single layer and cook for 3 minutes.

5. After 3 minutes, flip the scallops over and cook for a further 3 minutes until they are cooked through.

6. Garnish with chopped parsley before serving.

Marinated Swordfish Skewers

Serves 4

Prep time: 30 minutes / Cook time: 6-8 minutes

Ingredients

- 455 g filleted swordfish
- 60 ml avocado oil
- 2 tablespoons freshly squeezed lemon juice
- 1 tablespoon minced fresh parsley
- 2 teaspoons Dijon mustard
- Sea salt and freshly ground black pepper, to taste
- 85 g cherry tomatoes

Preparation instructions

1. Cut the fish into 1½-inch chunks, picking out any remaining bones.

2. In a large bowl, whisk together the oil, lemon juice, parsley, and Dijon mustard. Season to taste with salt and pepper. Add the fish and toss to coat the pieces. Cover and marinate the fish chunks in the refrigerator for 30 minutes.

3. Remove the fish from the marinade. Thread the fish and cherry tomatoes on 4 skewers, alternating as you go.

4. Set the air fryer to 204°C. Place the skewers in the air fryer basket and air fry for 3 minutes. Flip the skewers and cook for 3 to 5 minutes longer, until the fish is cooked through and

an instant-read thermometer reads 60°C.

Crispy Prawn Cakes

Serves 4

Prep time: 15 minutes / Cook time: 10 minutes

Ingredients

- 500g raw prawns, peeled and deveined
- 1 egg
- 1 tbsp cornflour
- 2 cloves garlic, minced
- 1 red chilli, finely chopped
- 2 spring onions, finely chopped
- 1 tsp fish sauce
- 1 tsp soy sauce
- 1 tsp sesame oil
- 1/4 tsp black pepper
- 50g panko breadcrumbs
- Cooking spray

Preparation instructions

1. Preheat the air fryer to 190°C.

2. In a food processor, pulse the prawns until they are finely chopped.

3. In a bowl, whisk the egg and cornflour together.

4. Add the chopped prawns, garlic, chilli, spring onions, fish sauce, soy sauce, sesame oil, and black pepper to the egg mixture. Mix well.

5. Divide the mixture into 8 portions and shape each portion into a patty.

6. Place the panko breadcrumbs on a plate and press each patty into the breadcrumbs, coating both sides.

7. Lightly spray the air fryer basket with cooking spray and place the prawn cakes inside.

8. Cook for 8-10 minutes, or until the prawn cakes are crispy and golden brown. 9. Serve with sweet chili sauce or a squeeze of lime juice.

Air Fryer Coconut Shrimp

Serves 4

Prep time: 15 minutes / Cook time: 8 minutes

Ingredients
- 500g raw shrimp, peeled and deveined
- 1/2 cup breadcrumbs
- 1/2 cup unsweetened shredded coconut
- 1/4 tsp salt
- 1/4 tsp black pepper
- 2 eggs, beaten

Preparation instructions
1. Preheat the air fryer to 200°C.
2. In a shallow dish, mix together the breadcrumbs, shredded coconut, salt, and black pepper.
3. Dip each shrimp in the beaten eggs, then coat with the breadcrumb mixture.
4. Place the shrimp in the air fryer basket, making sure they are not touching each other.
5. Cook for 8 minutes, flipping the shrimp halfway through, until they are golden brown and crispy. Serve with sweet chili sauce.

Air Fryer Salmon with Lemon and Dill

Serves 4

Prep time: 5 minutes / Cook time: 10 minutes

Ingredients
- 4 salmon fillets, skin on
- Salt and black pepper, to taste
- 1 lemon, sliced
- 2 tbsp chopped fresh dill

Preparation instructions

Preparation instructions
1. Preheat the air fryer to 400°F (200°C).
2. Season the salmon fillets with salt and black pepper, to taste.
3. Place the salmon fillets in the air fryer basket, skin side down.
4. Top each salmon fillet with a few slices of lemon and sprinkle with chopped dill.
5. Cook for 10 minutes, or until the salmon is cooked through and flakes easily with a fork.

Air Fryer Salmon Pattiesl

Serves 4

Prep time: 10 minutes / Cook time: 12 minutes

Ingredients
- 400g canned salmon, drained and flaked
- 30g breadcrumbs
- 40g chopped onion
- 1 egg, beaten
- 1 tbsp chopped fresh parsley
- 1 tbsp lemon juice
- 1/2 tsp salt
- 1/4 tsp black pepper
- Cooking spray

Preparation instructions
1. In a large mixing bowl, combine salmon, breadcrumbs, onion, egg, parsley, lemon juice, salt, and pepper.
2. Use your hands to form the mixture into 8 patties.
3. Preheat the air fryer to 200°C.

4. Spray the air fryer basket with cooking spray and add the patties in a single layer.

5. Air fry for 6 minutes, then flip and air fry for another 6 minutes, or until the patties are golden brown and cooked through.

Air Fryer Salmon Pattiesl

Serves 4

Prep time: 10 minutes / Cook time: 10 minutes

Ingredients

- 2 cod fillets (150-200g each)
- 2 tbsp unsalted butter, melted
- 1 tbsp fresh parsley, chopped
- 1 tbsp fresh chives, chopped
- 1 garlic clove, minced
- Salt and pepper to taste
- Lemon wedges for serving

Preparation instructions

1. Preheat your air fryer to 200°C.
2. In a small bowl, mix together melted butter, parsley, chives, garlic, salt and pepper.
3. Brush the herb butter mixture over the cod fillets.
4. Place the fillets in the air fryer basket, and cook for 8-10 minutes or until the fish is cooked through and flakes easily with a fork.
5. Serve with lemon wedges and enjoy!

Southern-Style Catfish

Serves 2

Prep time: 15 minutes / Cook time: 10 minutes

Ingredients

- 2 catfish fillets (150-200g each)
- 120ml buttermilk
- 60g cornmeal
- 1 tsp paprika
- 1/2 tsp garlic powder
- 1/2 tsp onion powder
- 1/4 tsp cayenne pepper
- Salt and pepper to taste
- Lemon wedges for serving

Preparation instructions

1. Preheat your air fryer to 200°C.
2. In a shallow dish, combine cornmeal, paprika, garlic powder, onion powder, cayenne pepper, salt and pepper.
3. Dip each catfish fillet in buttermilk, then dredge in the cornmeal mixture, making sure to coat the fish evenly.
4. Place the fillets in the air fryer basket, and cook for 8-10 minutes or until the fish is golden brown and cooked through.
5. Serve with lemon wedges and enjoy!

Panko Crab Sticks with Mayo Sauce

Serves 4

Prep time: 5 minutes / Cook time: 12 minutes

Ingredients

- Crab Sticks:
- 2 eggs
- 120 g plain flour
- 50 g panko bread crumbs
- 1 tablespoon Old Bay seasoning
- 455 g crab sticks
- Cooking spray
- Mayo Sauce:
- 115 g mayonnaise
- 1 lime, juiced
- 2 garlic cloves, minced

Preparation instructions

1. Preheat air fryer to 200°C.
2. In a bowl, beat the eggs. In a shallow bowl, place the flour. In another shallow bowl, thoroughly combine the panko bread crumbs and old bay seasoning.
3. Dredge the crab sticks in the flour, shaking off any excess, then in the beaten eggs, finally press them in the bread crumb mixture to coat well.
4. Arrange the crab sticks in the air fryer basket and spray with cooking spray.
5. Air fry for 12 minutes until golden brown. Flip the crab sticks halfway through the cooking time.
6. Meanwhile, make the sauce by whisking together the mayo, lime juice, and garlic in a small bowl.
7. Serve the crab sticks with the mayo sauce on the side.

Crispy salmon with lemon and dill

Serves 2

Prep time: 10 minutes / Cook time: 10 minutes

Ingredients

- 2 salmon fillets (150-200g each)
- 1/4 cup all-purpose flour
- 1 egg
- 1/2 cup panko breadcrumbs
- 1 tbsp fresh dill, chopped
- 1 tbsp lemon zest
- Salt and pepper to taste
Lemon wedges for serving

Preparation instructions

1. Preheat air fryer to 200°C.

2. Season the salmon fillets with salt and pepper.
3. Place the flour in a shallow dish, beat the egg in a separate shallow dish, and combine the panko breadcrumbs, dill, lemon zest, salt, and pepper in another shallow dish.
4. Dip each salmon fillet into the flour, then the egg, and finally coat with the breadcrumb mixture, pressing down lightly to ensure the mixture adheres to the salmon.
5. Place the fillets in the air fryer basket, and cook for 8-10 minutes or until the salmon is cooked through and the crust is golden and crispy.
6. Serve with lemon wedges and enjoy!

Prawns Scampi

Serves 4

Prep time: 8 minutes / Cook time: 8 minutes

Ingredients

- 4 tbsp salted butter or ghee
- 1 tbsp fresh lemon juice
- 1 tbsp minced garlic
- 2 tbsps red pepper flakes
- 455 g prawns (21 to 25 count), peeled and deveined
- 2 tbsps dry white wine or chicken broth
- 2 tbsps chopped fresh basil, plus more for sprinkling, or 1 teaspoon dried
- 1 tbsp chopped fresh chives, or 1 teaspoon dried

Preparation instructions

1. Place a baking pan in the air fryer basket. Set the air fryer to 164°C for 8 minutes (this will preheat the pan so the butter will melt faster).

2. Carefully remove the pan from the fryer and add the butter, lemon juice, garlic, and red pepper flakes. Place the pan back in the fryer.

3. Cook for 2 minutes, stirring once, until the butter has melted. (Do not skip this step; this is what infuses the butter with garlic flavor, which is what Makes it all taste so good.)

4. Carefully remove the pan from the fryer and add the prawns, broth, basil, and chives. Stir gently until the Ingredients are well combined.

5. Return the pan to the air fryer and cook for 5 minutes, stirring once.

6. Thoroughly stir the prawn mixture and let it rest for 1 minute on a wire rack. (This is so the prawns cook in the residual heat rather than getting overcooked and rubbery.)

7. Stir once more, sprinkle with additional chopped fresh basil, and serve.

Air Fryer Battered Fish

Serves 4

Prep time: 15 minutes / Cook time: 10-15 minutes

Ingredients

* 4 fish fillets (haddock, cod, or another white fish)
* 1/2 cup all-purpose flour
* 1 tsp baking powder
* 1/2 tsp salt
* 1/2 cup beer (lager or pale ale)
* 1 egg
* 1 tbsp olive oil
* Lemon wedges and tartar sauce, for serving

Preparation instructions

1. Preheat your air fryer to 200ºC.

2. In a mixing bowl, combine the flour, baking powder, and salt.

3. Beat the egg in a separate bowl and then add to the dry mixture.

4. Gradually stir in the beer until the batter is smooth.

5. Dip each fish fillet into the batter, coating both sides evenly.

6. Place the fillets in the air fryer basket and spray lightly with olive oil.

7. Cook for 10-15 minutes, until the fish is golden and crispy, and cooked through.

8. Serve with lemon wedges and tartar sauce.

Fish with Roasted Sweet Potatoes

Serves 2

Prep time: 10 minutes / Cook time: 20 minutes

Ingredients

* For the Fish:
* 2 white fish fillets (such as cod or haddock)
* 1/4 cup breadcrumbs
* 1/4 cup grated parmesan cheese
* 1/2 tsp garlic powder
* 1/2 tsp dried oregano
* 1/2 tsp dried basil
* Salt and black pepper to taste
* For the Roasted Sweet Potatoes:
* 1 large sweet potato, peeled and diced into 1 inch cubes
* 2 tbsp olive oil
* 1/2 tsp garlic powder
* Salt and black pepper to taste

Preparation instructions

1. Preheat your air fryer to 200ºC.

2. In a small bowl, combine breadcrumbs,

grated parmesan cheese, garlic powder, dried oregano, dried basil, salt, and black pepper.

3. Pat the fish fillets dry with paper towels.

4. Coat the fish fillets in the breadcrumb mixture, pressing the mixture onto the fish to ensure it sticks.

5. Place the fish fillets in the air fryer basket and spray lightly with cooking spray.

6. In a separate bowl, toss the diced sweet potatoes with olive oil, garlic powder, salt, and black pepper.

7. Place the seasoned sweet potatoes in the air fryer basket around the fish fillets.

8. Cook for 20 minutes, or until the fish is cooked through and the sweet potatoes are tender and crispy, stirring the sweet potatoes once halfway through cooking.

9. Serve the fish with the roasted sweet potatoes on the side. Enjoy!

Air Fryer Fish Tempura

Serves 4

Prep time: 15 minutes / Cook time: 10-12 minutes

Ingredients

- 4 white fish fillets, cut into chunks (400g)
- 60g all-purpose flour (60g)
- 60g cornstarch (60g)
- 1 teaspoon baking powder
- 1/2 teaspoon salt
- 120ml ice-cold water
- Cooking spray
- Lemon wedges, for serving

Preparation instructions

1. Preheat the air fryer to 190ºC.

2. In a medium bowl, whisk together the flour, cornstarch, baking powder, and salt.

3. Add the ice-cold water to the flour mixture and whisk until smooth.

4. Dip the fish chunks into the batter and shake off any excess.

5. Spray the air fryer basket with cooking spray.

6. Arrange the fish chunks in a single layer in the air fryer basket.

7. Spray the top of the fish with cooking spray.

8. Air fry the fish for 10-12 minutes, flipping halfway through, until golden brown and crispy.

9. Serve hot with lemon wedges.

Marinated Swordfish Skewers

Serves 4

Prep time: 30 minutes / Cook time: 6-8 minutes

Ingredients

- 455 g filleted swordfish
- 60 ml avocado oil
- 2 tablespoons freshly squeezed lemon juice
- 1 tablespoon minced fresh parsley
- 2 teaspoons Dijon mustard
- Sea salt and freshly ground black pepper, to taste
- 85 g cherry tomatoes

Preparation instructions

1. Cut the fish into 1½-inch chunks, picking out any remaining bones.

2. In a large bowl, whisk together the oil, lemon juice, parsley, and Dijon mustard. Season to taste with salt and pepper. Add the fish and toss to coat the pieces. Cover and marinate the fish chunks in the refrigerator for 30

minutes.

3. Remove the fish from the marinade. Thread the fish and cherry tomatoes on 4 skewers, alternating as you go.

4. Set the air fryer to 204°C. Place the skewers in the air fryer basket and air fry for 3 minutes. Flip the skewers and cook for 3 to 5 minutes longer, until the fish is cooked through and an instant-read thermometer reads 60°C.

Seasoned Breaded Prawns

Serves 4

Prep time: 15 minutes / Cook time: 10-15 minutes

Ingredients

- 2 teaspoons Old Bay seasoning, divided
- ½ teaspoon garlic powder
- ½ teaspoon onion powder
- 455 g large prawns, peeled and deveined, with tails on
- 2 large eggs
- 75 g whole-wheat panko bread crumbs
- Cooking spray

Preparation instructions

1. Preheat the air fryer to 192°C.
2. Spray the air fryer basket lightly with cooking spray.
3. In a medium bowl, mix together 1 teaspoon of Old Bay seasoning, garlic powder, and onion powder. Add the prawns and toss with the seasoning mix to lightly coat.
4. In a separate small bowl, whisk the eggs with 1 teaspoon water.
5. In a shallow bowl, mix together the remaining 1 teaspoon Old Bay seasoning and the panko

bread crumbs.

6. Dip each prawns in the egg mixture and dredge in the bread crumb mixture to evenly coat.

7. Place the prawns in the air fryer basket, in a single layer. Lightly spray the prawns with cooking spray. You many need to cook the prawns in batches.

8. Air fry for 10 to 15 minutes, or until the prawns is cooked through and crispy, shaking the basket at 5-minute intervals to redistribute and evenly cook.

9. Serve immediately.

Chilean Sea Bass with Olive Relish

Serves 2

Prep time: 10 minutes / Cook time: 10 minutes

Ingredients

- Olive oil spray
- 2 (170 g) Chilean sea bass fillets or other firm-fleshed white fish
- 3 tablespoons extra-virgin olive oil
- ½ teaspoon ground cumin
- ½ teaspoon kosher or coarse sea salt
- ½ teaspoon black pepper
- 60 g pitted green olives, diced
- 10 g finely diced onion
- 1 teaspoon chopped capers

Preparation instructions

1. Spray the air fryer basket with the olive oil spray. Drizzle the fillets with the olive oil and sprinkle with the cumin, salt, and pepper. Place the fish in the air fryer basket. Set the air fryer to 164°C for 10 minutes, or

until the fish flakes easily with a fork.

2. Meanwhile, in a small bowl, stir together the olives, onion, and capers.

3. Serve the fish topped with the relish.

Air Fryer Fish Cakes

Serves 4

Prep time: 20 minutes / Cook time: 15 minutes

Ingredients

- 300g cooked white fish, flaked
- 400g mashed potatoes
- 10g chopped fresh parsley
- 10g chopped fresh chives
- 60ml mayonnaise
- 1 tablespoon Dijon mustard
- 1 teaspoon garlic powder
- 1/2 teaspoon salt
- 1/4 teaspoon black pepper
- 60g all-purpose flour
- 2 eggs, beaten
- 150g panko breadcrumbs
- Cooking spray
- Lemon wedges, for serving

Preparation instructions

1. In a large bowl, combine the flaked fish, mashed potatoes, parsley, chives, mayonnaise, Dijon mustard, garlic powder, salt, and black pepper. Mix until well combined.

2. Form the mixture into 8-10 equal-sized patties.

3. Place the flour, beaten eggs, and panko breadcrumbs in separate shallow bowls.

4. Dredge each fish cake in the flour, shaking off any excess.

5. Dip the floured fish cake into the beaten eggs, making sure it is well coated.

6. Finally, coat the fish cake in the panko breadcrumbs, pressing lightly to help the breadcrumbs adhere.

7. Preheat the air fryer to 190°C.

8. Spray the air fryer basket with cooking spray.

9. Place the fish cakes in a single layer in the air fryer basket. Spray the top of the fish cakes with cooking spray.

10. Air fry the fish cakes for 12-15 minutes, flipping halfway through, until golden brown and crispy. Serve.

CHAPTER 4 PORK, BEEF AND LAMB

Mustard Herb Pork Tenderloin

Serves 5

Prep time: 5 minutes / Cook time: 25 minutes

Ingredients

- 60 ml mayonnaise
- 2 tablespoons Dijon mustard
- ½ teaspoon dried thyme
- ¼ teaspoon dried rosemary
- 1 (450 g) pork tenderloin
- ½ teaspoon salt
- ¼ teaspoon ground black pepper

Preparation instructions

1. In a small bowl, mix mayonnaise, mustard, thyme, and rosemary. Brush tenderloin with mixture on all sides, then sprinkle with salt and pepper on all sides.
2. Place tenderloin into ungreased air fryer basket. Adjust the temperature to 204°C and air fry for 20 minutes, turning tenderloin halfway through cooking. Tenderloin will be golden and have an internal temperature of at least 64°C when done.
3. Serve warm.

Chinese-Inspired Spareribs

Serves 4

Prep time: 30 minutes / Cook time: 8 minutes

Ingredients

- Oil, for spraying
- 340 g boneless pork spareribs, cut into 3-inch-long pieces
- 235 ml soy sauce
- 180 ml sugar
- 120 ml beef or chicken stock
- 60 ml honey
- 2 tablespoons minced garlic
- 1 teaspoon ground ginger
- 2 drops red food colouring (optional)

Preparation instructions

1. Line the air fryer basket with parchment and spray lightly with oil.
2. Combine the ribs, soy sauce, sugar, beef stock, honey, garlic, ginger, and food colouring (if using) in a large zip-top plastic bag, seal, and shake well until completely coated.
3. Refrigerate for at least 30 minutes.
4. Place the ribs in the prepared basket. Air fry at 192°C for 8 minutes, or until the internal temperature reaches 74°C.

Spicy Rump Steak

Serves 4

Prep time: 25 minutes / Cook time: 12-18 minutes

Ingredients

- 2 tablespoons salsa
- 1 tablespoon minced chipotle pepper or chipotle paste
- 1 tablespoon apple cider vinegar
- 1 teaspoon ground cumin
- ⅛ teaspoon freshly ground black pepper
- ⅛ teaspoon red pepper flakes
- 340 g rump steak, cut into 4 pieces and gently pounded to about ⅓ inch thick
- Cooking oil spray

Preparation instructions

1. In a small bowl, thoroughly mix the salsa, chipotle pepper, vinegar, cumin, black pepper, and red pepper flakes. Rub this mixture into both sides of each steak piece. Let stand for 15 minutes at room temperature.
2. Insert the crisper plate into the basket and place the basket into the unit. Preheat the unit by selecting AIR FRY, setting the temperature to 200°C, and setting the time to 3 minutes. Select START/STOP to begin.
3. Once the unit is preheated, spray the crisper plate with cooking oil. Working in batches, place 2 steaks into the basket.
4. Select AIR FRY, set the temperature to 200°C, and set the time to 9 minutes. Select START/STOP to begin.
5. After about 6 minutes, check the steaks. If a food thermometer inserted into the meat registers at least 64°C, they are done. If not, resume cooking.
6. When the cooking is done, transfer the steaks to a clean plate and cover with aluminum foil to keep warm. Repeat steps 3, 4, and 5 with the remaining steaks.
7. Thinly slice the steaks against the grain and serve.

Pork Burgers with Cabbage Salad

Serves 4

Prep time: 20 minutes / Cook time: 15 minutes

Ingredients

- 500g ground pork
- 1/2 onion, finely chopped
- 1/4 cup breadcrumbs
- 2 garlic cloves, minced
- 1 egg
- 1 tsp salt
- 1/2 tsp black pepper
- 4 brioche buns
- 4 lettuce leaves
- 4 slices of tomato
- 4 slices of cheddar cheese
- 1/4 head of cabbage, thinly sliced
- 2 tbsp olive oil
- 2 tbsp apple cider vinegar
- 1 tbsp honey
- 1/2 tsp salt
- 1/4 tsp black pepper

Preparation instructions

1. InIn a bowl, mix together the ground pork, onion, breadcrumbs, garlic, egg, salt, and black pepper. Mix well until all Ingredients are fully incorporated.
2. Form the mixture into four equal-sized

patties and place them into the air fryer basket.

3. Set the air fryer to 190°C and cook the pork burgers for 12-15 minutes, flipping them halfway through the cooking time.

4. While the burgers are cooking, make the cabbage salad. In a large bowl, whisk together the olive oil, apple cider vinegar, honey, salt, and black pepper.

5. Add the sliced cabbage to the bowl and toss well to coat in the dressing.

6. Once the burgers are done, remove them from the air fryer and let them rest for a few minutes.

7. To assemble the burgers, place a lettuce leaf on the bottom half of each brioche bun. Place a cooked pork burger on top of the lettuce and add a slice of tomato and cheddar cheese. Finish with a heaping spoonful of cabbage salad and the top half of the brioche bun.

8. Serve immediately and enjoy!

Pork Kebab with Rocket

Serves 4

Prep time: 20 minutes / Cook time: 10 minutes

Ingredients

- 500g pork loin, cut into 2cm cubes
- 1 red onion, cut into wedges
- 1 red pepper, cut into chunks
- 1 yellow pepper, cut into chunks
- 1 green pepper, cut into chunks
- 2 tbsp olive oil
- 1 tsp smoked paprika
- 1 tsp ground cumin
- 1 tsp ground coriander

- 1 tsp dried oregano
- Salt and pepper, to taste
- Rocket leaves, to serve

Preparation instructions

1. Preheat the air fryer to 180°C.

2. In a large bowl, mix together the olive oil, smoked paprika, ground cumin, ground coriander, dried oregano, salt and pepper.

3. Add the pork cubes to the bowl and toss to coat.

4. Thread the pork cubes, red onion wedges and pepper chunks onto skewers.

5. Place the skewers in the air fryer basket and cook for 8-10 minutes or until the pork is cooked through and the vegetables are tender.

6. Serve the kebabs with rocket leaves.

Air Fryer Steak with Garlic Butter

Serves 2

Prep time: 10 minutes / Cook time: 8-10 minutes

Ingredients

- 2 sirloin steaks (about 200g each)
- 1 tsp garlic powder
- 1 tsp smoked paprika
- 2 tbsp butter, softened
- Salt and pepper to taste

Preparation instructions

1. Preheat your air fryer to 200°C.

2. In a small mixing bowl, combine garlic powder, smoked paprika, salt, and pepper.

3. Season the steaks with the spice mixture, rubbing it all over.

4. Place the steaks in the air fryer basket and

cook for 4-5 minutes per side, depending on your desired level of doneness.

5. While the steaks are cooking, mix the softened butter with a pinch of salt and minced garlic.

6. Serve the steaks with a dollop of garlic butter on top.

Air Fryer Beef and Cheddar Stuffed Potatoes

Serves 4

Prep time: 10 minutes / Cook time: 45-50 minutes

Ingredients

- 4 large baking potatoes
- 500g ground beef
- 1 onion, chopped
- 1 red bell pepper, chopped
- 2 cloves garlic, minced
- 1 tsp dried oregano
- Salt and pepper to taste
- 100g shredded cheddar cheese

Preparation instructions

1. Preheat your air fryer to 200°C.
2. Pierce the potatoes several times with a fork.
3. Place the potatoes in the air fryer basket and cook for 45-50 minutes, or until they are tender.
4. In a frying pan, cook the ground beef over medium heat until browned.
5. Add the chopped onion, bell pepper, garlic, oregano, salt, and pepper to the pan and cook

Air Fryer Beef Empanadas

Serves 6

Prep time: 20 minutes / Cook time: 10 minutes

Ingredients

- 500g ground beef
- 1 onion, chopped
- 1 red bell pepper, chopped
- 2 cloves garlic, minced
- 2 tbsp tomato paste
- 2 tsp cumin
- 1 tsp chili powder
- Salt and pepper to taste
- 6 empanada pastry shells
- 1 egg, beaten

Preparation instructions

1. Preheat your air fryer to 180°C.
2. In a frying pan, cook the ground beef over medium heat until browned.
3. Add the chopped onion, bell pepper, garlic, tomato paste, cumin, chili powder, salt, and pepper to the pan and cook until the vegetables are softened.
4. Roll out the empanada pastry shells and cut them into circles.
5. Spoon the beef mixture onto the center of each circle.
6. Brush the edges of the pastry circles with beaten egg and fold them in half to form half-moon shapes.
7. Crimp the edges with a fork to seal.
8. Place the empanadas in the air fryer basket and cook for 8-10 minutes, or until golden brown.

Air Fryer Korean Beef Bowl

Serves 4

Prep time: 10 minutes / Cook time: 15 minutes

Ingredients

- 500g ground beef
- 1/2 cup soy sauce
- 1/4 cup brown sugar
- 2 tbsp sesame oil
- 1 tbsp minced garlic
- 1 tbsp grated ginger
- 1 tsp red pepper flakes
- Salt and pepper to taste
- Cooked rice, for serving
- Green onions, sliced, for garnish

Preparation instructions

1. Preheat the air fryer to 180°C.
2. In a bowl, whisk together the soy sauce, brown sugar, sesame oil, garlic, ginger, red pepper flakes, salt, and pepper.
3. In a frying pan, cook the ground beef over medium heat until browned.
4. Pour the sauce over the beef and cook for another 2-3 minutes.
5. Divide the beef mixture into bowls, and serve over cooked rice.
6. Garnish with sliced green onions.

70 British Haslet Duo

Serves 2

Prep time: 30 minutes / Cook time: 20-25 minutes

Ingredients

- 2 beef fillets (6-8 ounces each)
- Salt and pepper to taste
- 1 tbsp olive oil
- 1 sheet puff pastry
- 1 egg, beaten
- 1/2 cup mushrooms, finely chopped
- 2 cloves garlic, minced
- 2 tbsp butter
- 1 tbsp fresh thyme leaves

Preparation instructions

1. Preheat the air fryer to 200°C.
2. Season the beef fillets with salt and pepper.
3. In a pan, heat olive oil over medium-high heat and sear the beef fillets for 1-2 minutes on each side until browned. Remove the beef from the pan and set aside to cool.
4. In the same pan, melt butter and sauté the mushrooms and garlic until the moisture has evaporated and the mixture is slightly caramelized. Remove the mushroom mixture from heat and let it cool.
5. On a floured surface, roll out the puff pastry into a rectangle large enough to wrap around the beef fillets.
6. Spread the mushroom mixture over the puff pastry and sprinkle with thyme leaves.
7. Place the beef fillets on top of the mushroom mixture and wrap the puff pastry around the beef fillets, making sure to seal the edges.
8. Brush the beaten egg over the puff pastry to create a golden brown finish.
9. Place the Beef Wellington into the air fryer basket and cook for 20-25 minutes, or until the pastry is golden brown and the beef fillets are cooked to your desired level of doneness.
10. Remove the Beef Wellington from the air fryer and let it rest for a few minutes before slicing and serving.

Spicy Lamb Burger Topped With Herbed Yogurt

Serves 4

Prep time: 15 minutes / Cook time: 15 minutes

Ingredients

- 500g ground lamb
- 1/2 cup breadcrumbs
- 1 egg
- 1/4 cup chopped parsley
- 1/4 cup chopped cilantro
- 1 tbsp cumin powder
- 1 tbsp smoked paprika
- 1 tsp chili powder
- Salt and pepper to taste
- 4 burger buns
- 1 cup Greek yogurt
- 1/4 cup chopped mint
- 1/4 cup chopped dill
- Juice of 1/2 lemon

Preparation instructions

1. Preheat the air fryer to 200°C.
2. In a large mixing bowl, combine the ground lamb, breadcrumbs, egg, parsley, cilantro, cumin powder, smoked paprika, chili powder, salt, and pepper.
3. Mix everything together until well combined.
4. Divide the mixture into 4 portions and shape each portion into a patty.
5. Place the patties into the air fryer basket and cook for 10-12 minutes or until the internal temperature of the burgers reaches 160°

Rib-Eye Pork Ribs & Rosemary

Serves 2

Prep time: 10 minutes / Cook time: 30 minutes

Ingredients

- 2 rib-eye pork ribs (about 500g each)
- Salt and pepper to taste
- 1 tbsp olive oil
- 2 garlic cloves, minced
- 2 sprigs fresh rosemary

Preparation instructions

1. Preheat the air fryer to 180°C.
2. Season the rib-eye pork ribs with salt and pepper.
3. Drizzle olive oil over the pork ribs and rub it in, making sure that the ribs are well coated.
4. Add minced garlic to the pork ribs and rub it in as well.
5. Place the pork ribs into the air fryer basket.
6. Add the sprigs of fresh rosemary to the basket.
7. Cook the pork ribs in the air fryer for 30 minutes, flipping them halfway through the cooking time.
8. Check the internal temperature of the pork ribs to ensure they have reached at least 145°F (63°C).
9. Remove the pork ribs from the air fryer and let them rest for a few minutes before slicing and serving. Garnish with fresh rosemary sprigs if desired.

Meat Chops Duo(Pork and Lamb)

Serves 4

Prep time: 10 minutes / Cook time: 20 minutes

Ingredients

- 4 pork chops (about 200 g each)
- 4 lamb chops (about 150 g each)
- Salt and pepper to taste
- 2 tbsp olive oil

Preparation instructions

1. Preheat the air fryer to 190°C.
2. Season the pork chops and lamb chops with salt and pepper.
3. Drizzle olive oil over the meat and rub it in, making sure that the meat is well coated.
4. Place the meat chops into the air fryer basket.
5. Cook the meat chops in the air fryer for 20 minutes, flipping them halfway through the cooking time.
6. Check the internal temperature of the meat to ensure they have reached a safe temperature (145°F for pork and 160°F for lamb).
7. Remove the meat chops from the air fryer and let them rest for a few minutes before serving.

BBQ Baby Back Ribs

Serves 4

Prep time: 10 minutes / Cook time: 25 minutes

Ingredients

- 1 rack baby back ribs
- 30 ml olive oil
- 30 g BBQ seasoning
- Salt and pepper to taste
- 120 ml BBQ sauce

Preparation instructions

1. Preheat the air fryer to 180°C.
2. Remove the membrane from the back of the ribs and season with olive oil, BBQ seasoning, salt, and pepper.
3. Place the seasoned ribs in the air fryer basket and cook for 20 minutes.
4. Brush the BBQ sauce over the ribs and cook for an additional 5 minutes or until the internal temperature of the ribs reaches 75°C.
5. Remove the ribs from the air fryer and let them rest for 5 minutes before serving.

Air Fryer BBQ Pork Chops

Serves 4

Prep time: 10 minutes / Cook time: 15 minutes

Ingredients
- 500 g beef sirloin, cut into cubes
- 30 ml olive oil
- 30 g BBQ seasoning
- Salt and pepper to taste
- Wooden skewers, soaked in water for 30 minutes
- 120 ml BBQ sauce

Preparation instructions
1. Preheat the air fryer to 200°C.
2. Season the beef cubes with olive oil, BBQ seasoning, salt, and pepper.
3. Thread the beef cubes onto the skewers.
4. Place the skewers in the air fryer basket and cook for 10 minutes.
5. Brush the BBQ sauce over the skewers and cook for an additional 5 minutes or until the internal temperature of the beef reaches 63°C.
6. Remove the skewers from the air fryer and let them rest for 5 minutes before serving.

Sichuan Cumin Lamb

Serves 4

Prep time: 10 minutes / Cook time: 20 minutes

Ingredients
- 500 g lamb leg or shoulder, thinly sliced
- 30 ml vegetable oil
- 30 g cumin seeds
- 20 g Sichuan peppercorns
- 10 g chili flakes
- 5 g ginger powder
- 5 g garlic powder
- Salt to taste

Preparation instructions
1. Preheat the air fryer to 200°C.
2. In a small pan, toast the cumin seeds, Sichuan peppercorns, and chili flakes until fragrant, then grind them into a powder using a spice grinder or mortar and pestle.
3. Season the lamb slices with the ground spice mixture, ginger powder, garlic powder, and salt to taste.
4. Brush the lamb slices with vegetable oil and place them in the air fryer basket in a single layer.
5. Cook the lamb slices for 10 minutes, flipping them halfway through cooking.
6. After 10 minutes, increase the temperature to 220°C and cook the lamb slices for an additional 5-10 minutes until they are crispy and browned.
7. Serve hot with rice or noodles. Enjoy!

Sumptuous Pizza Tortilla Rolls

Serves 4

Prep time: 10 minutes / Cook time: 6 minutes

Ingredients

- 1 teaspoon butter
- ½ medium onion, slivered
- ½ red or green pepper, julienned
- 110 g fresh white mushrooms, chopped
- 120 ml pizza sauce
- 8 flour tortillas
- 8 thin slices wafer-thinham
- 24 pepperoni slices
- 235 ml shredded Mozzarella cheese
- Cooking spray

Preparation instructions

1. Preheat the air fryer to 200°C.
2. Put butter, onions, pepper, and mushrooms in a baking pan. Bake in the preheated air fryer for 3 minutes. Stir and cook 3 to 4 minutes longer until just crisp and tender. Remove pan and set aside.
3. To assemble rolls, spread about 2 teaspoons of pizza sauce on one half of each tortilla. Top with a slice of ham and 3 slices of pepperoni. Divide sautéed vegetables among tortillas and top with cheese.
4. Roll up tortillas, secure with toothpicks if needed, and spray with oil.
5. Put 4 rolls in air fryer basket and air fry for 4 minutes. Turn and air fry 4 minutes, until heated through and lightly browned.
6. Repeat step 4 to air fry remaining pizza rolls.
7. Serve immediately.

Teriyaki Lamb Chop with Chilli

Serves 4

Prep time: 10 minutes / Cook time: 15 minutes

Ingredients

- 8 lamb chops
- 30 ml soy sauce
- 30 ml mirin
- 30 ml sake
- 30 g brown sugar
- 5 g ginger, grated
- 1-2 red chilies, sliced
- 2 garlic cloves, minced
- 10 ml sesame oil
- Salt and pepper to taste

Preparation instructions

1. Preheat the air fryer to 200°C.
2. In a small bowl, mix together the soy sauce, mirin, sake, brown sugar, ginger, garlic, sesame oil, and sliced chilies.
3. Season the lamb chops with salt and pepper on both sides.
4. Dip each lamb chop in the teriyaki sauce, making sure it is well-coated.
5. Place the lamb chops in the air fryer basket in a single layer.
6. Cook the lamb chops for 10 minutes, flipping them halfway through cooking.
7. After 10 minutes, brush the remaining teriyaki sauce over the lamb chops and cook for an additional 5 minutes until they are caramelized and cooked through.
8. Remove the lamb chops from the air fryer and let them rest for 5 minutes before serving.
9. Serve hot with steamed rice and your favorite vegetables. Enjoy!

CHAPTER 5   TOFU & TEMPEH

Sesame Taj Tofu

Serves 4

Prep time: 5 minutes / Cook time: 25 minutes

Ingredients

* 1 block firm tofu, pressed and cut into 1-inch thick cubes
* 2 tablespoons soy sauce
* 2 teaspoons toasted sesame seeds
* 1 teaspoon rice vinegar
* 1 tablespoon cornflour

Preparation instructions

1. Preheat the air fryer to 200°C.
2. Add the tofu, soy sauce, sesame seeds, and rice vinegar in a bowl together and mix well to coat the tofu cubes. Then cover the tofu in cornflour and put it in the air fryer basket.
3. Air fry for 25 minutes, giving the basket a shake at five-minute intervals to ensure the tofu cooks evenly.
4. Serve immediately.

Air Fryer Tofu and Vegetable Skewers

Serves 4

Prep time: 15 minutes / Cook time: 15 minutes

Ingredients

* 1 block firm tofu, pressed and drained
* 1 red onion, chopped into bite-sized pieces
* 1 red pepper, chopped into bite-sized pieces
* 1 zucchini, chopped into bite-sized pieces
* 30 ml olive oil
* 5 g smoked paprika
* 5 g garlic powder
* 5 g onion powder

Salt and pepper to taste

Preparation instructions

1. Insert crisper plates in both drawers. Preheat the air fryer to 200°C.
2. Cut the tofu block into bite-sized pieces.
3. In a small bowl, mix together the olive oil, smoked paprika, garlic powder, onion powder, salt, and pepper.
4. Thread the tofu and vegetables onto skewers.
5. Brush the skewers with the spice mixture.
6. Place the skewers in the air fryer basket in a single layer.
7. Cook the skewers for 12-15 minutes, flipping them halfway through cooking, until the tofu and vegetables are cooked through and tender.
8. Serve hot with rice or a salad. Enjoy!

Air Fryer Tofu Banh Mi

Serves 4

Prep time: 15 minutes / Cook time: 10 minutes

Ingredients

- 1 block firm tofu, pressed and drained
- 2 tbsp soy sauce
- 2 tbsp rice vinegar
- 2 tbsp brown sugar
- 1 tsp garlic powder
- 1 tsp onion powder
- 1 baguette, sliced
- 4 tbsp mayonnaise
- 1 carrot, shredded
- 1 cucumber, sliced
- 1 jalapeno, sliced

Cilantro, for garnish

Preparation instructions

1. Preheat the air fryer to 200°C.
2. Cut the tofu block into slices.
3. In a small bowl, mix together the soy sauce, rice vinegar, brown sugar, garlic powder, and onion powder.
4. Dip each tofu slice into the soy sauce mixture, making sure it is well-coated.
5. Place the tofu slices in the air fryer basket in a single layer.
6. Cook the tofu for 8-10 minutes, flipping them halfway through cooking, until they are crispy and browned.
7. Assemble the banh mi by spreading mayonnaise on the sliced baguette, then adding the tofu, shredded carrot, cucumber, and jalapeno slices.
8. Garnish with cilantro and serve. Enjoy!

Air Fryer Tofu Scramble:

Serves 2

Prep time: 10 minutes / Cook time: 10 minutes

Ingredients

- 1 block firm tofu, pressed and drained
- 15 ml olive oil
- 1/2 onion, diced
- 1/2 red bell pepper, diced
- 2 cloves garlic, minced
- 5 g turmeric
- Salt and pepper to taste
- 15 g nutritional yeast
- Fresh parsley, for garnish

Preparation instructions

1. Preheat the air fryer to 180°C.
2. Crumble the tofu into small pieces.
3. In a pan, heat the olive oil over medium heat. Add the onion, bell pepper, and garlic, and cook until softened.
4. Add the crumbled tofu to the pan and stir to combine with the vegetables.
5. Sprinkle turmeric, salt, and pepper over the tofu mixture and continue cooking for a few minutes until the tofu is lightly browned.
6. Transfer the tofu scramble to the air fryer basket and cook for 5-7 minutes until crispy.
7. Remove from the air fryer and sprinkle with nutritional yeast and fresh parsley.

Tofu with Honey Garlic Sauce

Serves 4

Prep time: 10 minutes / Cook time: 20 minutes

Ingredients
- 1 block of extra-firm tofu, drained and pressed (about 400g)
- 30g cornstarch
- 60ml vegetable oil
- 60ml honey
- 45ml soy sauce
- 2 cloves garlic, minced
- 1/2 teaspoon ginger, minced
- 60ml water
- Salt and pepper to taste
- Green onions, chopped (for garnish)

Preparation instructions
1. Cut the tofu into bite-sized cubes and toss them in cornstarch until evenly coated.
2. Preheat the air fryer to 190°C.
3. Place the tofu cubes in the air fryer basket and spray with oil.
4. Air fry the tofu for 10 minutes, shaking the basket halfway through, until golden and crispy.
5. While the tofu is cooking, make the sauce by whisking together honey, soy sauce, garlic, ginger, water, salt and pepper in a small saucepan.
6. Bring the sauce to a simmer over medium heat and cook for 2-3 minutes until thickened.
7. Toss the crispy tofu in the sauce until coated evenly.
8. Garnish with chopped green onions and serve hot over rice or noodles.

Air Fryer BBQ Tempeh

Serves 2

Prep time: 10 minutes / Cook time: 15 minutes

Ingredients
- 200g tempeh, sliced into 1/2-inch strips
- 60ml BBQ sauce
- 15ml vegetable oil
- 1/2 teaspoon smoked paprika
- 1/2 teaspoon garlic powder
- Salt and pepper to taste

Preparation instructions
1. Preheat the air fryer to 190°C.
2. In a bowl, whisk together the BBQ sauce, vegetable oil, smoked paprika, garlic powder, salt, and pepper.
3. Add the sliced tempeh to the bowl and toss to coat evenly.
4. Place the tempeh in the air fryer basket and cook for 8 minutes.
5. Flip the tempeh and cook for an additional 7 minutes until crispy and browned.
6. Serve hot with additional BBQ sauce for dipping.

Air Fryer Buffalo Tempeh Wraps

Serves 2-3

Prep time: 15 minutes / Cook time: 10 minutes

Ingredients

- 1/2 tsp black pepper
- 1 block of tempeh, sliced into thin strips (200g)
- 60ml all-purpose flour
- 1 tsp garlic powder
- 1 tsp paprika
- 1/2 tsp salt
- 2 tbsp buffalo sauce
- 2 tbsp olive oil
- 4-6 large tortilla wraps
- 60ml ranch dressing
- 30g chopped celery
- 30g chopped carrots

30g chopped red onio

Preparation instructions

1. Preheat the air fryer to 190°C.
2. In a shallow dish, mix together the flour, garlic powder, paprika, salt, and black pepper.
3. Dip the tempeh strips into the flour mixture, shaking off any excess.
4. Place the tempeh strips into the air fryer basket and spray them with olive oil.
5. Air fry for 8-10 minutes, flipping the tempeh strips halfway through, until they are crispy and golden brown.
6. In a separate bowl, mix together the buffalo sauce and remaining olive oil.
7. Once the tempeh strips are done, toss them in the buffalo sauce mixture until they are evenly coated.
8. To assemble the wraps, spread a spoonful of ranch dressing onto each tortilla wrap.
9. Add a few strips of buffalo tempeh, along with the chopped celery, carrots, and red onion.
10. Fold in the sides of the tortilla and then roll it up tightly. Repeat with the remaining tortilla wraps and filling.
11. Serve the wraps immediately and enjoy!

Sweet and Sour Sauce

Serves 2-3

Prep time: 15 minutes / Cook time: 12 minutes

Ingredients

- 200g firm tofu, pressed and sliced into cubes
- 2 tbsp cornstarch
- Salt and pepper, to taste
- 2 tbsp vegetable oil
- 1/4 cup ketchup
- 1/4 cup rice vinegar
- 2 tbsp brown sugar
- 2 tbsp soy sauce
- 1 tsp garlic powder
- 1 tsp onion powder
- 1 tsp ginger powder
- 1 tbsp cornstarch, mixed with 1 tbsp water

Preparation instructions

1. Preheat the air fryer to 190°C.
2. In a shallow dish, mix together the cornstarch, salt, and pepper.
3. Dip the tofu cubes into the cornstarch mixture, shaking off any excess.
4. Place the tofu cubes into the air fryer basket and spray them with vegetable oil.

5. Air fry for 10-12 minutes, shaking the basket occasionally, until they are crispy and golden brown.

6. In a small bowl, whisk together the peanut butter, soy sauce, rice vinegar, honey, sesame oil, garlic powder, and red pepper flakes.

7. Slowly add warm water, whisking continuously until the sauce reaches your desired consistency.

8. Once the tofu cubes are done, transfer them to a plate and drizzle with the peanut sauce.

9. Serve immediately.

BBQ Sauce

Serves 3

Prep time: 10 minutes / Cook time: 10-12 minutes

Ingredients
- 200g tempeh, sliced into thin strips
- 2 tbsp olive oil
- 2 tbsp BBQ sauce
- 1 tbsp soy sauce
- 1 tsp smoked paprika
- 1 tsp garlic powder
- Salt and pepper, to taste

Preparation instructions
1. Preheat the air fryer to 190°C.
2. In a small bowl, whisk together the olive oil, BBQ sauce, soy sauce, smoked paprika, garlic powder, salt, and pepper.
3. Dip the tempeh strips into the sauce mixture, coating them evenly.
4. Place the tempeh strips into the air fryer basket and air fry for 10-12 minutes, flipping them halfway through.

5. Once the tempeh strips are crispy and golden brown, transfer them to a plate and drizzle with any remaining sauce.

6. Serve immediately.

Air Fryer Sweet Chili Tempeh

Serves 2

Prep time: 10 minutes / Cook time: 15 minutes

Ingredients
- 1 block of tempeh
- 2 tbsp sweet chili sauce
- 1 tbsp soy sauce
- 1 tsp garlic powder
- 1 tbsp chopped green onions (optional)

Preparation instructions
1. Preheat the air fryer to 190°C.
2. Cut the tempeh into bite-sized pieces.
3. In a bowl, mix together the sweet chili sauce, soy sauce, and garlic powder.
4. Add the tempeh to the bowl and toss to coat.
5. Place the tempeh in the air fryer basket and cook for 15 minutes, flipping halfway through.
6. Sprinkle chopped green onions over the tempeh before serving (optional).

Air Fryer Caesar Salad with Tempeh Croutons

Serves 2

Prep time: 10 minutes / Cook time: 15 minutes

Ingredients

- 1 block of tempeh
- 2 tbsp olive oil
- 1 tbsp nutritional yeast
- 1 tsp garlic powder
- Salt and pepper, to taste
- 4 cups chopped romaine lettuce
- Vegan Caesar dressing, to taste
- Vegan parmesan cheese, to taste

Preparation instructions

1. Preheat the air fryer to 190°C.
2. Cut the tempeh into small cubes.
3. In a bowl, mix together the olive oil, nutritional yeast, garlic powder, salt, and pepper.
4. Add the tempeh to the bowl and toss to coat.
5. Place the tempeh in the air fryer basket and cook for 15 minutes, shaking the basket halfway through.
6. To assemble the salad, divide the romaine lettuce between two plates.
7. Drizzle vegan Caesar dressing over the lettuce and top with the tempeh croutons.
8. Sprinkle vegan parmesan cheese over the salad before serving.

Air Fryer Tofu Tacos

Serves 2

Prep time: 10 minutes / Cook time: 15 minutes

Ingredients

- 1 block of firm tofu, drained and pressed
- 1 tbsp taco seasoning
- 1 tbsp vegetable oil
- 4 corn tortillas
- 1/2 cup shredded lettuce
- 1/2 cup diced tomatoes
- 1/4 cup chopped cilantro
- 2 tbsp chopped green onions
- Lime wedges, for serving

Preparation instructions

1. Preheat the air fryer to 190°C.
2. Cut the tofu into small cubes.
3. In a bowl, toss the tofu with the taco seasoning and vegetable oil.
4. Place the tofu in the air fryer basket and cook for 10 minutes, shaking the basket halfway through.
5. Warm the tortillas in a pan or in the microwave.
6. Divide the tofu between the tortillas.
7. Top with shredded lettuce, diced tomatoes, cilantro, and green onions.
8. Squeeze lime wedges over the tacos before serving.

CHAPTER 6 VEGETABLE RECIPES

Baked Sweet Potato Falafel

Serves 4

Prep time: 15 minutes / Cook time: 25 minutes

Ingredients

- 2 medium sweet potatoes, peeled and chopped
- 1 can chickpeas, drained and rinsed
- 1/4 cup flour
- 1 small onion, finely chopped
- 2 garlic cloves, minced
- 2 tbsp chopped fresh parsley
- 2 tbsp olive oil
- 1 tsp ground cumin
- 1/2 tsp ground coriander
- Salt and pepper to tast

Preparation instructions

1. Preheat the oven to 190°C.
2. Line a baking sheet with parchment paper.
3. Place the sweet potatoes in a large bowl and microwave for 5 minutes, or until tender.
4. Add the chickpeas to the bowl and mash them together with the sweet potatoes using a potato masher or fork.
5. Add the flour, onion, garlic, parsley, olive oil, cumin, coriander, salt, and pepper to the bowl and mix well.
6. Form the mixture into small balls (about 2 tbsp each) and place them on the prepared baking sheet.
7. Bake for 20-25 minutes, or until the falafels are golden brown and crispy on the outside.
8. Serve the falafels in a pita pocket with your favorite toppings, such as hummus, tzatziki, sliced tomatoes, and cucumber. Enjoy!

Roasted Vegetables

Serves 4

Prep time: 10 minutes / Cook time: 20 minutes

Ingredients

- 500g mixed vegetables (e. g. broccoli, cauliflower, peppers, courgette, etc.), cut into bite-sized pieces
- 1 tablespoon olive oil
- 1/2 teaspoon salt
- 1/2 teaspoon garlic powder
- 1/4 teaspoon black pepper
- Cooking spray

Preparation instructions

1. Preheat the air fryer to 200°C.
2. In a bowl, toss the vegetables with olive oil, salt, garlic powder, and black pepper.
3. Spray the air fryer basket with cooking spray.
4. Arrange the vegetables in a single layer in the basket.
5. Air fry for 10 minutes, then shake the basket and air fry for another 5-10 minutes, until the vegetables are tender and golden brown.

Marinara Pepperoni Mushroom Pizza

Serves 4

Prep time: 10 minutes / Cook time: 10 minutes

Ingredients

- 225g of pizza dough
- 120ml of marinara sauce
- 120g of shredded mozzarella cheese
- 30g of sliced pepperoni
- 30g of sliced mushrooms 1 teaspoon of olive oil
- Salt and pepper
- Italian seasoning

Preparation instructions

1. Preheat the air fryer to 190°C.
2. Roll out the pizza dough on a floured surface to your desired size and thickness.
3. Transfer the dough onto a greased air fryer basket or tray.
4. Brush the dough with olive oil. Spread marinara sauce over the pizza dough, leaving a small border around the edge.
5. Sprinkle shredded mozzarella cheese over the tomato sauce.
6. Arrange sliced pepperoni and sliced mushrooms on top of the cheese.
7. Sprinkle some salt, pepper, and Italian seasoning over the pizza.
8. Place the pizza in the preheated air fryer and cook for 10-12 minutes, or until the crust is golden brown and the cheese is melted and bubbly.
9. Remove the pizza from the air fryer and let it cool for a few minutes before slicing and serving.

Spinach and Swiss Frittata with Mushrooms

Serves 4

Prep time: 10 minutes / Cook time: 20 minutes

Ingredients

- Olive oil cooking spray
- 8 large eggs
- ½ teaspoon salt
- ½ teaspoon black pepper
- 1 garlic clove, minced
- 475 ml fresh baby spinach
- 110 g baby mushrooms, sliced
- 1 shallot, diced
- 120 ml shredded Swiss cheese, divided
- Hot sauce, for serving (optional)

Preparation instructions

1. Preheat the air fryer to 182°C. Lightly coat the inside of a 6-inch round cake pan with olive oil cooking spray.
2. In a large bowl, beat the eggs, salt, pepper, and garlic for 1 to 2 minutes, or until well combined.
3. Fold in the spinach, mushrooms, shallot, and 60 ml the Swiss cheese.
4. Pour the egg mixture into the prepared cake pan, and sprinkle the remaining 60 ml Swiss over the top.
5. Place into the air fryer and bake for 18 to 20 minutes, or until the eggs are set in the center.
6. Remove from the air fryer and allow to cool for 5 minutes. Drizzle with hot sauce (if using) before serving.

Swordfish Skewers with Caponata

Serves 2

Prep time: 15 minutes / Cook time: 20 minutes

Ingredients

- 280 g small Italian aubergine, cut into 1-inch pieces
- 170 g cherry tomatoes
- 3 spring onions, cut into 2 inches long
- 2 tablespoons extra-virgin olive oil, divided
- Salt and pepper, to taste
- 340 g skinless swordfish steaks, 1¼ inches thick, cut into 1-inch pieces
- 2 teaspoons honey, divided
- 2 teaspoons ground coriander, divided
- 1 teaspoon grated lemon zest, divided
- 1 teaspoon juice
- 4 (6-inch) wooden skewers
- 1 garlic clove, minced
- ½ teaspoon ground cumin
- 1 tablespoon chopped fresh basil

Preparation instructions

1. Preheat the air fryer to 204ºC.
2. Toss aubergine, tomatoes, and spring onions with 1 tablespoon oil, ¼ teaspoon salt, and ⅛ teaspoon pepper in bowl; transfer to air fryer basket. Air fry until aubergine is softened and browned and tomatoes have begun to burst, about 14 minutes, tossing halfway through cooking. Transfer vegetables to cutting board and set aside to cool slightly.
3. Pat swordfish dry with paper towels. Combine 1 teaspoon oil, 1 teaspoon honey, 1 teaspoon coriander, ½ teaspoon lemon zest, ⅛ teaspoon salt, and pinch pepper in a clean bowl. Add swordfish and toss to coat. Thread swordfish onto skewers, leaving about ¼ inch between each piece (3 or 4 pieces per skewer).
4. Arrange skewers in air fryer basket, spaced evenly apart. (Skewers may overlap slightly.) Return basket to air fryer and air fry until swordfish is browned and registers 140ºF (60ºC), 6 to 8 minutes, flipping and rotating skewers halfway through cooking.
5. Meanwhile, combine remaining 2 teaspoons oil, remaining 1 teaspoon honey, remaining 1 teaspoon coriander, remaining ½ teaspoon lemon zest, lemon juice, garlic, cumin, ¼ teaspoon salt, and ⅛ teaspoon pepper in large bowl. Microwave, stirring once, until fragrant, about 30 seconds. Coarsely chop the cooked vegetables, transfer to bowl with dressing, along with any accumulated juices, and gently toss to combine. Stir in basil and season with salt and pepper to taste. Serve skewers with caponata.

Easy Greek Briami (Ratatouille)

Serves 6

Prep time: 15 minutes / Cook time: 40 minutes

Ingredients

- 2 Maris Piper potatoes, cubed
- 100 g plum tomatoes, cubed
- 1 aubergine, cubed
- 1 courgette, cubed
- 1 red onion, chopped
- 1 red pepper, chopped
- 2 garlic cloves, minced
- 1 teaspoon dried mint

- 1 teaspoon dried parsley
- 1 teaspoon dried oregano
- ½ teaspoon salt
- ½ teaspoon black pepper
- ¼ teaspoon red pepper flakes
- 80 ml olive oil
- 1 (230 g) can tomato paste
- 65 ml vegetable stock
- 65 ml water

Preparation instructions

1. Preheat the air fryer to 160°C.
2. In a large bowl, combine the potatoes, tomatoes, aubergine, courgette onion, bell pepper, garlic, mint, parsley, oregano, salt, black pepper, and red pepper flakes.
3. In a small bowl, mix together the olive oil, tomato paste, stock, and water.
4. Pour the oil-and-tomato-paste mixture over the vegetables and toss until everything is coated.
5. Pour the coated vegetables into the air fryer basket in an even layer and roast for 20 minutes. After 20 minutes, stir well and spread out again. Roast for an additional 10 minutes, then repeat the process and cook for another 10 minutes.

Air Fryer Brussel Sprouts

Serves 4

Prep time: 10 minutes / Cook time: 15 minutes

Ingredients

- 500g Brussel sprouts, trimmed and halved
- 2 tablespoons olive oil
- 1 teaspoon garlic powder
- 1/2 teaspoon onion powder
- 1/2 teaspoon paprika

- Salt and pepper to taste

Preparation instructions

1. Preheat the air fryer to 375°F (190°C).
2. In a bowl, toss the Brussel sprouts with olive oil, garlic powder, onion powder, paprika, salt, and pepper.
3. Place the Brussel sprouts in the air fryer basket in a single layer.
4. Cook for 8 minutes, then shake the basket and cook for an additional 7 minutes or until tender and lightly browned.
5. Serve immediately as a side dish or use in your favorite recipes.

Air Fryer Cauliflower Wings

Serves 4

Prep time: 10 minutes / Cook time: 20 minutes

Ingredients

- 1 large head of cauliflower, cut into bite-sized florets
- 1 cup all-purpose flour
- 1 cup unsweetened almond milk
- 1 teaspoon garlic powder
- 1 teaspoon smoked paprika
- 1/2 teaspoon salt
- 1/4 teaspoon black pepper
- 1/2 cup hot sauce
- 2 tablespoons melted butter or vegan butter

Preparation instructions

1. Preheat the air fryer to 190°C.
2. In a bowl, whisk together the flour, almond milk, garlic powder, smoked paprika, salt, and black pepper to make a batter.
3. Dip the cauliflower florets into the batter to coat them evenly.

4. Place the coated cauliflower florets in the air fryer basket in a single layer.

5. Cook for 10 minutes, then flip the cauliflower florets over and cook for an additional 10 minutes or until crispy and golden brown.

6. In a separate bowl, mix together the hot sauce and melted butter.

7. Toss the cooked cauliflower florets in the hot sauce mixture until evenly coated.

8. Serve immediately with your favorite dipping sauce.

Air Fryer Cauliflower Fried Rice

Serves 4

Prep time: 10 minutes / Cook time: 15 minutes

Ingredients

- 1 large head of cauliflower, grated into rice-sized pieces
- 1 tablespoon sesame oil
- 1 tablespoon soy sauce
- 1 teaspoon garlic powder
- 1 teaspoon ginger powder
- 1 cup frozen mixed vegetables
- 2 eggs, beaten (optional for non-vegan)
- Salt and pepper to taste

Preparation instructions

1. Preheat the air fryer to 190°C.

2. In a bowl, mix together the grated cauliflower, sesame oil, soy sauce, garlic powder, and ginger powder.

3. Place the cauliflower mixture in the air fryer basket in a single layer.

4. Cook for 7 minutes, then stir in the frozen mixed vegetables.

5. Cook for an additional 5 minutes or until the vegetables are tender and the cauliflower is lightly browned.

6. Push the cauliflower mixture to one side of the air fryer basket and pour the beaten eggs into the other side.

7. Scramble the eggs in the air fryer basket until cooked through, then stir them into the cauliflower mixture.

8. Season with salt and pepper to taste and serve immediately.

Air Fryer Asparagus and Mushroom Skewers

Serves 4

Prep time: 10 minutes / Cook time: 15 minutes

Ingredients

- 400g asparagus, trimmed
- 100g sliced mushrooms
- 2 tablespoons olive oil
- 1 teaspoon garlic powder
- 1/2 teaspoon salt
- 1/4 teaspoon black peppe

Preparation instructions

1. Preheat the air fryer to190°C.

2. In a bowl, whisk together the olive oil, garlic powder, salt, and black pepper.

3. Thread the asparagus and mushroom slices onto skewers.

4. Brush the skewers with the seasoned oil mixture to coat them evenly.

5. Place the skewers in the air fryer basket in a single layer.

6. Cook for 8 minutes, then flip the skewers over and cook for an additional 7 minutes

or until the vegetables are tender and lightly browned.

7. Serve immediately as a side dish or appetizer.

Creamy Cheese Stuffed Courgette Boats

Serves 4

Prep time: 10 minutes / Cook time: 25 minutes

Ingredients

- 4 courgettes, halved lengthwise
- 100g cream cheese
- 50g grated cheddar cheese
- 2 tablespoons chopped fresh parsley
- 1 tablespoon chopped fresh thyme
- 1/2 teaspoon garlic powder
- 1/2 teaspoon salt
- 1/4 teaspoon black pepper
- 1 tablespoon olive oil

Preparation instructions

1. Preheat the air fryer to190°C.
2. Using a spoon, scoop out the seeds and flesh from the courgette halves to create a hollow space.
3. In a bowl, mix together the cream cheese, cheddar cheese, parsley, thyme, garlic powder, salt, and black pepper until well combined.
4. Spoon the cheese mixture into the courgette boats, filling them evenly.
5. Brush the tops of the courgette boats with olive oil.
6. Place the stuffed courgette boats on a baking sheet lined with parchment paper.
7. Bake for 20-25 minutes, or until the courgettes are tender and the cheese is

melted and lightly browned.

8. Serve hot as a side dish or a light main dish.

Roasted Beetroot with Dill and Garlic

Serves 4

Prep time: 10 minutes / Cook time: 40 minutes

Ingredients

- 600g beetroots, peeled and chopped into bite-size pieces
- 2 cloves garlic, minced
- 2 tablespoons chopped fresh dill
- 2 tablespoons olive oil
- 1/2 teaspoon salt
- 1/4 teaspoon black pepper

Preparation instructions

1. Preheat the air fryer to200°C.
2. In a large bowl, mix together the chopped beetroot, minced garlic, chopped dill, olive oil, salt, and black pepper until well combined.
3. Spread the beetroot mixture in a single layer on a baking sheet lined with parchment paper.
4. Roast in the preheated oven for 35-40 minutes, or until the beetroots are tender and lightly browned.
5. Remove from the oven and let cool for a few minutes before serving.
6. Serve hot as a side dish or a light vegetarian main dish.
7. Enjoy your roasted beetroot with dill and garlic!

Air-Fried Brussels Sprouts Salad

Serves 4

Prep time: 10 minutes / Cook time: 10 minutes

Ingredients

- 450g Brussels sprouts, trimmed and halved
- 2 tbsp olive oil
- Salt and pepper to taste
- 60g dried cranberries
- 30g chopped walnuts
- 60g crumbled feta cheese
- 2 tbsp balsamic vinegar
- 1 tbsp honey
- 1 tbsp Dijon mustard

Preparation instructions

1. Preheat the air fryer to190°C.
2. In a bowl, toss the Brussels sprouts with olive oil, salt, and pepper.
3. Place the Brussels sprouts in the air fryer basket in a single layer.
4. Air fry the Brussels sprouts for 10 minutes, shaking the basket once or twice during cooking.
5. In a separate bowl, whisk together the balsamic vinegar, honey, and Dijon mustard to make the dressing.
6. Once the Brussels sprouts are done, let them cool slightly before assembling the salad.
7. In a large bowl, combine the air-fried Brussels sprouts with the dried cranberries, chopped walnuts, and crumbled feta cheese.
8. Drizzle the dressing over the salad and toss to combine.

Air-Fried Chickpea Salad

Serves 4

Prep time: 10 minutes / Cook time: 15 minutes

Ingredients

- 1 can (400g) chickpeas, drained and rinsed
- 1 tbsp olive oil
- 1 tsp cumin
- Salt and pepper to taste
- 1 red bell pepper, diced
- 1 small red onion, diced60 g chopped fresh parsley
- 60 g crumbled feta cheese
- 2 tbsp lemon juice
- 1 tbsp honey
- 1 tbsp Dijon mustard

Preparation instructions

1. Preheat the air fryer to190°C.
2. In a bowl, toss the chickpeas with olive oil, cumin, salt, and pepper.
3. Place the chickpeas in the air fryer basket in a single layer.
4. Air fry the chickpeas for 15 minutes, shaking the basket once or twice during cooking.
5. In a separate bowl, whisk together the lemon juice, honey, and Dijon mustard to make the dressing.
6. Once the chickpeas are done, let them cool slightly before assembling the salad.
7. In a large bowl, combine the air-fried chickpeas with the diced red bell pepper, diced red onion, chopped fresh parsley, and crumbled feta cheese.
8. Drizzle the dressing over the salad and toss to combine.

Fig, Chickpea, and Rocket Salad

Serves 4

Prep time: 15 minutes / Cook time: 20minutes

Ingredients

- 8 fresh figs, halved
- 250 g cooked chickpeas
- 1 teaspoon crushed roasted cumin seeds
- 4 tablespoons balsamic vinegar
- 2 tablespoons extra-virgin olive oil, plus more for greasing
- Salt and ground black pepper, to taste
- 40 g rocket, washed and dried

Preparation instructions

1. Preheat the air fryer to 192°C.
2. Cover the air fryer basket with aluminum foil and grease lightly with oil. Put the figs in the air fryer basket and air fry for 10 minutes.
3. In a bowl, combine the chickpeas and cumin seeds.
4. Remove the air fried figs from the air fryer and replace with the chickpeas. Air fry for 10 minutes. Leave to cool.
5. In the meantime, prepare the dressing. Mix the balsamic vinegar, olive oil, salt and pepper.
6. In a salad bowl, combine the rocket with the cooled figs and chickpeas.
7. Toss with the sauce and serve.

Blackened Courgette with Kimchi-Herb Sauce

Serves 4

Prep time: 15 minutes / Cook time: 10 minutes

Ingredients

- 4 medium courgettes, sliced into rounds
- 30 ml olive oil
- 5 g smoked paprika
- 5 g garlic powder
- Salt and pepper to taste
- 60 g kimchi
- 60 ml Greek yogurt
- 30 g chopped fresh parsley
- 15 g chopped fresh mint
- 15 ml lemon juice
- 15 ml honey

Preparation instructions

1. Preheat the air fryer to190°C.
2. In a bowl, toss the courgette rounds with olive oil, smoked paprika, garlic powder, salt, and pepper.
3. Place the courgette rounds in the air fryer basket in a single layer.
4. Air fry the courgette rounds for 10 minutes, shaking the basket once or twice during cooking.
5. While the courgettes are cooking, prepare the sauce. In a blender or food processor, combine the kimchi, Greek yogurt, chopped parsley, chopped mint, lemon juice, and honey. Blend until smooth.
6. Once the courgette rounds are done, transfer them to a plate and drizzle the sauce over the top.
7. Serve immediately and enjoy!

Carrot and Sugar Snap Pea Salad

Serves 4

Prep time: 10 minutes / Cook time: 5 minutes

Ingredients

- 300 g carrots, peeled and cut into thin strips
- 200 g sugar snap peas
- 30 ml olive oil
- 15 ml rice vinegar
- 5 g honey
- 5 g Dijon mustard
- Salt and pepper to taste
- 30 g chopped fresh cilantro
- 15 g sesame seeds, toasted

Preparation instructions

1. Preheat the air fryer to 200°C.
2. In a bowl, toss the carrots and sugar snap peas with olive oil and season with salt and pepper.
3. Place the vegetables in the air fryer basket in a single layer.
4. Air fry the vegetables for 5 minutes, shaking the basket once during cooking.
5. While the vegetables are cooking, prepare the dressing. In a small bowl, whisk together the rice vinegar, honey, Dijon mustard, and salt and pepper to taste.
6. Once the vegetables are done, transfer them to a serving bowl and drizzle with the dressing.
7. Sprinkle the chopped cilantro and toasted sesame seeds over the top.
8. Serve immediately and enjoy!

Tomato Salad with Sauce

Serves 4

Prep time: 10 minutes / Cook time: 5 minutes

Ingredients

- 500 g cherry tomatoes, halved
- 30 ml olive oil
- Salt and pepper to taste
- 15 ml balsamic vinegar
- 5 g honey
- 5 g Dijon mustard
- 1 garlic clove, minced
- 15 g chopped fresh basil

Preparation instructions

1. Preheat your air fryer to 200°C.
2. In a bowl, toss the cherry tomatoes with olive oil and season with salt and pepper.
3. Place the tomatoes in the air fryer basket in a single layer.
4. Air fry the tomatoes for 5 minutes, shaking the basket once during cooking.
5. While the tomatoes are cooking, prepare the sauce. In a small bowl, whisk together the balsamic vinegar, honey, Dijon mustard, minced garlic, and salt and pepper to taste.
6. Once the tomatoes are done, transfer them to a serving bowl and drizzle with the sauce.
7. Sprinkle the chopped basil over the top.
8. Serve immediately and enjoy!

Lemon Asparagus Fries

Serves 4

Prep time: 10 minutes / Cook time: 10 minutes

Ingredients

- 500 g asparagus, trimmed
- 30 ml olive oil
- Salt and pepper to taste
- Zest of 1 lemon
- 60 g panko breadcrumbs
- 30 g grated Parmesan cheese
- 5 g garlic powder
- 2 eggs, beaten

Preparation instructions

1. Preheat your air fryer to 200°C.
2. In a bowl, toss the asparagus with olive oil and season with salt, pepper, and lemon zest.
3. In a separate bowl, mix together the panko breadcrumbs, Parmesan cheese, and garlic powder.
4. Dip the asparagus spears in the beaten eggs and then coat them in the breadcrumb mixture.
5. Place the asparagus fries in the air fryer basket in a single layer.
6. Air fry the asparagus for 10 minutes, shaking the basket once during cooking.
7. Once done, serve hot with your favorite dipping sauce.

Hasselback Potatoes with Chive Pesto

Serves 2

Prep time: 10 minutes / Cook time: 40 minutes

Ingredients

- 2 medium Maris Piper potatoes
- 5 tablespoons olive oil
- coarse sea salt and freshly ground black pepper, to taste
- 10 g roughly chopped fresh chives
- 2 tablespoons packed fresh flat-leaf parsley leaves
- 1 tablespoon chopped walnuts
- 1 tablespoon grated Parmesan cheese
- 1 teaspoon fresh lemon juice
- 1 small garlic clove, peeled
- 60 g sour cream

Preparation instructions

1. Place the potatoes on a cutting board and lay a chopstick or thin-handled wooden spoon to the side of each potato. Thinly slice the potatoes crosswise, letting the chopstick or spoon handle stop the blade of your knife, and stop ½ inch short of each end of the potato. Rub the potatoes with 1 tablespoon of the olive oil and season with salt and pepper.
2. Place the potatoes, cut-side up, in the air fryer and air fry at 192°C until golden brown and crisp on the outside and tender inside, about 40 minutes, drizzling the insides with 1 tablespoon more olive oil and seasoning with more salt and pepper halfway through.
3. Meanwhile, in a small blender or food processor, combine the remaining 3

tablespoons olive oil, the chives, parsley, walnuts, Parmesan, lemon juice, and garlic and purée until smooth. Season the chive pesto with salt and pepper.

4. Remove the potatoes from the air fryer and transfer to plates. Drizzle the potatoes with the pesto, letting it drip down into the grooves, then dollop each with sour cream and serve hot.

Garlicky Potato Vegetable Medley

Serves 4

Prep time: 10 minutes / Cook time: 20 minutes

Ingredients

- 500 g baby potatoes, halved
- 250 g cherry tomatoes
- 250 g green beans, trimmed
- 30 ml olive oil
- 3 garlic cloves, minced
- Salt and pepper to taste
- 5 g dried thyme
- 15 g chopped fresh parsley

Preparation instructions

1. Preheat your air fryer to 200°C.
2. In a bowl, toss the baby potatoes, cherry tomatoes, and green beans with olive oil, garlic, salt, pepper, and dried thyme.
3. Place the vegetables in the air fryer basket in a single layer.
4. Air fry the vegetables for 20 minutes, shaking the basket once during cooking.
5. Once the vegetables are cooked and tender, transfer them to a serving dish.
6. Garnish with chopped fresh parsley and

serve hot as a side dish or as a vegetarian main dish. Enjoy!

Spicy tofu and vegetable stir-fry

Serves 8

Prep time: 15 minutes / Cook time: 20 minutes

Ingredients

- 1 tablespoon vegetable oil
- 400g firm tofu, pressed and cubed
- 1 red bell pepper, sliced
- 1 green bell pepper, sliced
- 1 small onion, sliced
- 1 small zucchini, sliced
- 1 small carrot, sliced
- 3 cloves garlic, minced
- 1 tablespoon cornstarch
- 2 tablespoons water
- 2 tablespoons soy sauce
- 1 tablespoon sriracha or hot sauce
- Salt and pepper, to taste
- Cooked rice or noodles, for serving

Preparation instructions

1. Preheat the air fryer to 200°C.
2. In a large bowl, whisk together the cornstarch, water, soy sauce, sriracha, salt, and pepper. Add the cubed tofu and toss until well coated.
3. Place the tofu cubes in the air fryer basket and air fry for 10-12 minutes, or until crispy and golden brown. Set aside.
4. In a large skillet, heat the vegetable oil over medium-high heat. Add the garlic and cook for 1-2 minutes, or until fragrant.
5. Add the sliced bell peppers, onion, zucchini, and carrot to the skillet. Cook for 5-7 minutes, or until the vegetables are tender and slightly caramelized.

6. Add the air-fried tofu to the skillet and stir until well combined.

7. Serve the stir-fry over cooked rice or noodles.

Vegan stuffed bell peppers

Serves 4

Prep time: 20 minutes / Cook time: 25-30 minutes

Ingredients

- 4 large bell peppers
- 1 tablespoon olive oil
- 1 small onion, chopped
- 3 cloves garlic, minced
- 1 medium zucchini, diced
- 1 medium carrot, diced
- 150g cooked brown rice
- 150g cooked black beans
- 75g corn kernels
- 120ml tomato sauce
- 1 teaspoon ground cumin
- 1 teaspoon smoked paprika
- Salt and pepper, to taste
- Vegan shredded cheese, for topping (optional)

Preparation instructions

1. Preheat the air fryer to 180°C.

2. Cut off the tops of the bell peppers and remove the seeds and membranes. Set aside.

3. In a large skillet, heat the olive oil over medium-high heat. Add the onion and garlic and cook until fragrant and tender, about 3-4 minutes.

4. Add the zucchini and carrot and cook for an additional 5-7 minutes, or until the vegetables are tender.

5. Add the cooked brown rice, black beans, corn, tomato sauce, cumin, smoked paprika, salt, and pepper to the skillet. Stir until well combined and cook for another 2-3 minutes.

6. Stuff the bell peppers with the vegetable and rice mixture.

7. Place the stuffed bell peppers in the air fryer basket and air fry for 20-25 minutes, or until the peppers are tender and the filling is heated through.

8. If desired, sprinkle some vegan shredded cheese on top of the stuffed bell peppers and air fry for an additional 2-3 minutes, or until the cheese is melted and bubbly.

Air-fried roasted root vegetables

Serves 4

Prep time: 10 minutes / Cook time: 15-20 minutes

Ingredients

- 1 large sweet potato, peeled and cubed
- 1 large parsnip, peeled and cubed
- 1 large carrot, peeled and cubed
- 1 small red onion, sliced
- 2 tablespoons olive oil
- 1 teaspoon garlic powder
- 1 teaspoon paprika
- 1 teaspoon dried thyme
- Salt and pepper, to taste

Preparation instructions

1. Preheat the air fryer to 200°C.

2. In a large bowl, toss the cubed sweet potato, parsnip, and carrot with the 3.sliced red onion, olive oil, garlic powder, paprika, dried thyme, salt, and pepper until well coated.

4. Place the vegetables in the air fryer basket and air fry for 15-20 minutes, 5.or until the vegetables are tender and slightly caramelized.

6. Serve the roasted root vegetables as a side dish or as a main dish with a salad.

Beef and Mango Skewers

Serves 4

Prep time: 20 minutes / Cook time: 12 minutes

Ingredients

- 450g beef sirloin, cut into 1-inch cubes
- 1 large mango, peeled and cut into 1-inch cubes
- 1 red bell pepper, seeded and cut into 1-inch pieces
- 1 yellow onion, cut into 1-inch pieces
- 2 tbsp olive oil
- 2 tbsp soy sauce
- 2 tbsp honey
- 1 tbsp chili powder
- Salt and pepper to taste
- 8 skewers

Preparation instructions

1. Preheat your air fryer to 200°C.
2. In a large bowl, whisk together the olive oil, soy sauce, honey, chili powder, salt, and pepper.
3. Add the beef cubes to the bowl and toss to coat evenly.
4. Thread the beef, mango, red pepper, and onion pieces onto the skewers, alternating between each ingredient.
5. Place the skewers in the air fryer basket and cook for 6 minutes.
6. Remove the basket and turn the skewers over.
7. Cook for an additional 6 minutes or until the beef is cooked to your desired level of doneness and the vegetables are tender and slightly charred.
8. Serve hot and enjoy!

Porridge Bread

Serves 6-8

Prep time: 10 minutes / Cook time: 35-40 minutes

Ingredients

- 200 g rolled oats
- 200 g wholemeal flour
- 1 tsp baking soda
- 1 tsp salt
- 300 ml buttermilk

Preparation instructions

1. Preheat your air fryer to 180°C.
2. In a large bowl, mix together the rolled oats, wholemeal flour, baking soda, and salt.
3. Pour in the buttermilk and stir well to combine.
4. Grease a 7-inch (18 cm) round cake pan and transfer the dough to the pan.
5. Smooth the top of the dough with a spatula and sprinkle with additional rolled oats if desired.
6. Place the pan in the air fryer basket and cook for 35-40 minutes or until the bread is golden brown and a toothpick inserted into the center comes out clean.
7. Remove the pan from the air fryer and let the bread cool for a few minutes before slicing and serving.

Cheese Quiche

Serves 6-8

Prep time: 20 minutes / Cook time: 25-30 minutes

Ingredients

- 1 pie crust
- 4 eggs
- 200 ml heavy cream
- 100 g grated cheddar cheese
- 1/2 onion, chopped
- Salt and pepper to taste

Preparation instructions

1. Preheat your air fryer to 180°C.
2. Roll out the pie crust and line a 7-inch (18 cm) round cake pan with it.
3. In a large bowl, whisk together the eggs, heavy cream, salt, and pepper.
4. Add the grated cheddar cheese and chopped onion to the bowl and stir to combine.
5. Pour the egg mixture into the pie crust.
6. Place the pan in the air fryer basket and cook for 25-30 minutes or until the quiche is set and golden brown on top.
7. Remove the pan from the air fryer and let the quiche cool for a few minutes before slicing and serving.

Okra Chips with Lemon Mayonnaise

Serves 2-4

Prep time: 15 minutes / Cook time: 10-12 minutes

Ingredients

- 225 g fresh okra, trimmed and sliced into thin rounds
- 30 g all-purpose flour
- 30 g cornmeal
- 1 tsp paprika
- 1 tsp garlic powder
- Salt and pepper to taste
- 1 egg, beaten
- Cooking spray
- Lemon wedges for serving

Preparation instructions

1. Preheat your air fryer to 200°C.
2. In a shallow dish, whisk together the flour, cornmeal, paprika, garlic powder, salt, and pepper.
3. In another shallow dish, beat the egg.
4. Dip the okra rounds into the beaten egg, then dredge them in the flour mixture to coat.
5. Place the coated okra rounds in a single layer in the air fryer basket.
6. Lightly spray the okra rounds with cooking spray.
7. Cook for 10-12 minutes or until the okra is crispy and golden brown, flipping them over halfway through cooking.
8. While the okra is cooking, make the Lemon Mayonnaise by whisking together the mayonnaise, lemon juice, lemon zest, salt, and pepper in a small bowl.
9. Serve the Okra Chips hot with the Lemon Mayonnaise and lemon wedges on the side

Cinnamon Sugar Snack Mix

Serves 6

Prep time: 5 minutes / Cook time: 5 minutes

Ingredients

- 100 g rice cereal squares
- 100 g oat cereal
- 60 g melted butter

- 50 g granulated sugar
- 1 tbsp ground cinnamon

Preparation instructions

1. Preheat your air fryer to 150°C.
2. In a large mixing bowl, combine the rice cereal squares and oat cereal.
3. In a separate small mixing bowl, whisk together the melted butter, granulated sugar, and ground cinnamon.
4. Pour the butter mixture over the snack mix and stir to coat.
5. Transfer the snack mix to the air fryer basket in a single layer.
6. Cook for 5 minutes, stirring halfway through cooking.
7. Allow the Cinnamon Sugar Snack Mix to cool completely before serving.

Mozzarella Sticks

Serves 4

Prep time: 20 minutes / Cook time: 6-8 minutes

Ingredients

- 12 sticks of string cheese
- 1/2 cup all-purpose flour
- 2 large eggs
- 2 tbsp water
- 1 cup Italian-seasoned breadcrumbs
- Cooking spray

Preparation instructions

1. Cut each string cheese stick in half crosswise to make 24 pieces.
2. In a shallow bowl, whisk together the flour and a pinch of salt.
3. In a separate shallow bowl, whisk together the eggs and water.

4. In a third shallow bowl, place the breadcrumbs.
5. Dip each piece of string cheese in the flour mixture, then in the egg mixture, and then coat with the breadcrumbs, pressing to adhere.
6. Place the coated string cheese pieces in a single layer in the air fryer basket.
7. Spray the tops of the mozzarella sticks with cooking spray.
8. Air fry at 200°C for 6-8 minutes, until golden brown and crispy.
9. Serve hot with your favorite dipping sauce.

Greek Potato Skins with Feta

Serves 4

Prep time: 15 minutes / Cook time: 1h

Ingredients

- 4 large baking potatoes (about 1 kg)
- 60 ml olive oil
- 1 teaspoon dried oregano
- 1/2 teaspoon garlic powder
- 1/4 teaspoon salt
- 1/4 teaspoon black pepper
- 113 g crumbled feta cheese
- 60 ml chopped fresh parsley

Preparation instructions

1. Preheat the oven to 200°C. Scrub the potatoes clean, prick them all over with a fork, and place them on a baking sheet. Bake for 45-50 minutes or until the potatoes are tender.
2. Remove the potatoes from the oven and let them cool for a few minutes. Cut the potatoes in half lengthwise and scoop out the insides, leaving about 1/4 inch of potato in the skin.

3. In a small bowl, mix together the olive oil, oregano, garlic powder, salt, and pepper. Brush the mixture over the inside and outside of each potato skin.

4. Place the potato skins back onto the baking sheet, skin side down. Sprinkle the crumbled feta cheese over each skin.

5. Bake for 10-15 minutes or until the cheese is melted and bubbly.

6. Garnish with chopped parsley and serve hot.

Bacon-Wrapped Shrimp and Jalapeño

Serves 4

Prep time: 20 minutes / Cook time: 10-15 minutes

Ingredients

* 18 large shrimp, peeled and deveined
* 6 jalapeño peppers, seeded and cut into 18 pieces
* 9 slices of bacon, cut in half
* 1/4 cup brown sugar
* 1/2 teaspoon garlic powder
* 1/2 teaspoon smoked paprika
* 1/4 teaspoon salt
* Toothpicks

Preparation instructions

1. Preheat your air fryer to 200°C. Line a baking sheet with parchment paper.

2. In a small bowl, mix together the brown sugar, garlic powder, smoked paprika, and salt.

3. Cut each slice of bacon in half. Take a piece of jalapeño and wrap it with a half slice of bacon. Then wrap a shrimp around the bacon-wrapped jalapeño and secure it with a toothpick. Repeat with the remaining shrimp, jalapeño, and bacon.

4. Place the bacon-wrapped shrimp and jalapeño on the prepared baking sheet. Sprinkle the brown sugar mixture over the top of each one.

5. Bake for 10-15 minutes or until the bacon is crispy and the shrimp is cooked through.

6. Remove from the oven and let cool for a few minutes before serving. Discard the toothpicks and serve hot.

Potato Pancakes

Serves 4

Prep time: 12 minutes / Cook time: 20 minutes

Ingredients

* 500 g baby potatoes, halved
* 4 large potatoes, peeled and grated (800 g)
* 1 small onion, grated
* 2 eggs, beaten
* 30g all-purpose flour
* 1/2 teaspoon salt
* 1/4 teaspoon black pepper
* 60ml vegetable oil

Preparation instructions

1. Preheat your air fryer to 200°C.

2. In a large bowl, combine the grated potatoes, grated onion, beaten eggs, flour, salt, and pepper. Mix well until everything is evenly combined.

3. Heat the vegetable oil in a large skillet over medium-high heat.

4. Drop spoonfuls of the potato mixture into the skillet, flattening each one slightly with the back of a spoon. Cook for 4-5 minutes on each side or until golden brown and crispy.

5. Remove the potato pancakes from the skillet and place them on a paper towel-lined plate to drain off any excess oil.

6. Repeat with the remaining potato mixture, adding more oil to the skillet as needed.

7. Serve the potato pancakes hot with your favorite toppings, such as sour cream, applesauce, or green onions.

Bruschetta with Tomato and Basil

Serves 4-6

Prep time: 10 minutes / Cook time: 5minutes

Ingredients

- 4 slices of ciabatta bread
- 4 medium tomatoes, diced
- 2 cloves of garlic, minced
- 1 tbsp extra-virgin olive oil
- 1 tbsp balsamic vinegar
- Salt and pepper to taste
- Fresh basil leaves

Preparation instructions

1. Preheat the air fryer to 200°C.
2. Slice the bread into 1 cm thick slices and brush them with olive oil.
3. Toast the bread in the oven for 5 minutes or until golden brown.
4. In a bowl, mix together the diced tomatoes, minced garlic, olive oil, balsamic vinegar, salt and pepper.
5. Spoon the tomato mixture onto the toasted bread slices.
6. Garnish with fresh basil leaves.
7. Serve immediately.

Bean Chips with Homemade Mayo Dip

Serves 4

Prep time: 10 minutes / Cook time: 10 minutes

Ingredients

- Bean Chips:
- 400g can of black beans, drained and rinsed
- 2 tbsp olive oil
- 1 tsp smoked paprika
- 1 tsp garlic powder
- 1 tsp onion powder
- Salt and pepper to taste
- Homemade Mayo Dip:
- 1/2 cup mayonnaise
- 1 tbsp lemon juice
- 1 tbsp Dijon mustard
- 1 clove garlic, minced
- Salt and pepper to taste

Preparation instructions

1. Preheat the air fryer to 200°C. Line a baking sheet with parchment paper.
2. In a bowl, mix together the black beans, olive oil, smoked paprika, garlic powder, onion powder, salt and pepper.
3. Spread the bean mixture evenly on the baking sheet.
4. Bake for 10-12 minutes or until crispy and golden brown.
5. While the bean chips are cooking, make the mayo dip.
6. In a small bowl, mix together the mayonnaise, lemon juice, Dijon mustard, garlic, salt and pepper until smooth.
7. Serve the bean chips hot with the homemade mayo dip on the side.

Air Fryer Pita Chips with Herbs and Olive Oil

Serves 4

Prep time: 5 minutes / Cook time: 5 minutes

Ingredients

- 4 pita breads
- 1 tbsp olive oil
- Salt to taste
- Optional: dried herbs such as oregano, thyme or rosemary

Preparation instructions

1. Preheat the air fryer to 180°C.
2. Cut the pita bread into triangles or wedges.
3. In a bowl, toss the pita bread with olive oil, salt and dried herbs if using.
4. Place the pita bread in the air fryer basket in a single layer.
5. Cook for 4-5 minutes, flipping halfway through, or until the pita chips are crispy and golden brown.
6. Remove from the air fryer and let cool for a few minutes.
7. Serve with your favourite dip, such as hummus or tzatziki.

Tricolour Vegetable Skewers with Oregano Oil

Serves 4

Prep time: 20 minutes / Cook time: 10-12 minutes

Ingredients

- 1 red bell pepper
- 1 yellow bell pepper
- 1 green bell pepper
- 1 red onion
- 1 courgette (zucchini)
- 1 tbsp olive oil
- 1 tsp dried oregano
- Salt and pepper to taste
- Wooden skewers, soaked in water for at least 30 minutes

Preparation instructions

1. Preheat the grill or BBQ to medium-high heat.
2. Cut the bell peppers and courgette into 1-inch pieces.
3. Cut the red onion into quarters and separate the layers.
4. Thread the vegetables onto the skewers, alternating the colours.
5. In a small bowl, mix together the olive oil, oregano, salt and pepper.
6. Brush the vegetable skewers with the oil mixture.
7. Grill the kebabs for 10-12 minutes, turning occasionally, or until the vegetables are tender and slightly charred.
8. Remove the kebabs from the grill and let them cool for a few minutes before serving.

Roasted Grape and Honey Dip with Cream Cheese

Serves 4

Prep time: 10 minutes / Cook time: 15 minutes

Ingredients

- 500g seedless red grapes
- 1 tbsp olive oil
- 1/4 tsp salt
- 1/4 tsp black pepper
- 1/2 tsp dried thyme
- 200g cream cheese, softened

- 2 tbsp honey
- 2 tbsp chopped fresh parsley
- Toasted baguette slices, crackers or pita chips, for serving

Preparation instructions

1. Preheat the air fryer to 200°C.
2. In a bowl, toss the grapes with olive oil, salt, pepper and thyme.
3. Place the grapes in the air fryer basket in a single layer.
4. Cook for 12-15 minutes, shaking the basket halfway through, or until the grapes are caramelized and slightly softened.
5. In a separate bowl, mix together the cream cheese and honey until smooth.
6. Fold in the roasted grapes and chopped parsley.
7. Transfer the dip to a serving bowl and garnish with additional parsley if desired.
8. Serve with toasted baguette slices, crackers or pita chips.

Savory Sausage and Cheese Cobbler

Serves 4

Prep time: 20 minutes / Cook time: 40 minutes

Ingredients

- 6 sausages (pork, beef or vegetarian)
- 2 tbsp olive oil
- 1 onion, chopped
- 2 cloves garlic, minced
- 1 red bell pepper, chopped
- 1 green bell pepper, chopped
- 1 tsp dried thyme
- 1 tsp dried oregano
- 1/2 tsp salt

- 1/2 tsp black pepper
- 400g can chopped tomatoes
- 200g self-raising flour
- 100g unsalted butter, chilled and cubed
- 100g mature cheddar cheese, grated
- 1 tsp dried parsley
- 1 egg, beaten
- 100ml milk

Preparation instructions

1. Preheat the air fryer to 200°C.
2. In a large frying pan, cook the sausages over medium-high heat until browned on all sides.
3. Remove the sausages from the pan and cut them into 1-inch pieces.
4. In the same pan, add olive oil, onion and garlic and cook until softened, about 5 minutes.
5. Add the chopped bell peppers, thyme, oregano, salt and black pepper and cook for another 5 minutes.
6. Add the chopped tomatoes and cooked sausages to the pan and stir to combine.
7. Transfer the sausage mixture to an ovenproof casserole dish.
8. In a mixing bowl, combine the self-raising flour, butter, grated cheese and dried parsley. Rub the mixture together with your fingers until it resembles breadcrumbs.
9. In a separate bowl, whisk together the beaten egg and milk. Pour the egg mixture into the dry Ingredients and stir until just combined.
10. Drop spoonfuls of the cobbler dough on top of the sausage mixture. Bake the cobbler for 25-30 minutes, or until the cobbler is golden brown and the sausage mixture is hot and bubbly.
11. Remove the cobbler from the oven and let it cool for a few minutes before serving.

CHAPTER 8   DESSERTS

American vanilla pancakes

Serves 4 pancakes

Prep time: 5 minutes / Cook time: 20 minutes

Ingredients
- 65g oat flour
- 3/4 tsp (3g) baking powder
- 1/4 tsp (1g) kosher salt
- 1 large egg
- 125 ml milk, whole
- 15g butter, melted
- 5 g golden syrup
- 4 drops of vanilla extract
- Olive oil cooking spray
- Toppings
- Raspberries
- Blueberries
- Golden syrup, Optional

Preparation instructions
1. In a medium bowl, whisk flour, baking powder, and salt.
2. In a separate medium bowl, whisk egg, milk, butter, golden syrup, and vanilla.
3. Fold dry Ingredients into egg mixture until just combined.
4. Grease a 15cm pie dish with cooking spray, then add one-quarter of batter.
5. Place dish in an air-fryer basket.
6. Cook at 205C until pancake is puffed and lightly golden, about 3 minutes.
7. Repeat with remaining batter.
8. Top pancakes with sliced fruit and drizzle with golden syrup if desired. Enjoy!

Lava cake with vanilla ice cream

Serves 3 cakes

Prep time: 10 minutes / Cook time: 3 minutes

Ingredients
- 75g milk chocolate chips
- 75g unsalted butter
- 1 egg
- A pinch of salt
- 40g plain flour
- Side
- Vanilla ice cream

Preparation instructions
1. Place a bowl with the chocolate and butter on top of the hot water bath.
2. Stir as the heat melts the mixture until smooth consistency.
3. Remove the bowl from the fire.
4. Beat the egg in a small bowl and add it to the chocolate mixture. Stir well.
5. Add in salt and flour and stir well till smooth.
6. Add a coat of butter to your air fryer containers to aid easy removal of your cakes later, and add the mixture to your containers.
7. Preheat the air fryer to 160C for 5 mins and cook for about 2 to 3 mins.
8. Remove it from the air fryer once you see that the top is cooked and looks solid.
9. Remove from the air fryer, flip it over, add the vanilla ice cream on the side or top and enjoy!

Mango Cupcakes

Serves : 12 cupcakes

Prep time: 20 minutes / Cook time: 20 minutes

Ingredients

For the cupcakes:
- 180g all-purpose flour
- 1 1/2 tsp baking powder
- 1/4 tsp salt
- 113g unsalted butter, softened
- 150g granulated sugar
- 2 large eggs
- 1 tsp vanilla extract
- 120g pureed mango
- 60ml milkPreparation instructions

For the frosting:
- 113g unsalted butter, softened
- 250g confectioners' sugar
- 60g pureed mango
- 1/2 tsp vanilla extract

Preparation instructions

1. Preheat the air fryer to 180°C. Line a 12-cup muffin tin with paper liners.
2. In a medium bowl, whisk together the flour, baking powder and salt.
3. In a large mixing bowl, cream together the butter and sugar until light and fluffy.
4. Add the eggs one at a time, mixing well after each addition. Stir in the vanilla extract and mango puree.
5. Gradually add the flour mixture to the butter mixture, alternating with the milk, and mix until just combined.
3. Divide the batter evenly among the prepared muffin cups, filling each cup about 2/3 full.
7. Bake for 18-20 minutes, or until a toothpick inserted into the center of a cupcake comes out clean.
8. Remove the cupcakes from the oven and let them cool in the tin for 5 minutes before transferring them to a wire rack to cool completely.
9. To make the frosting, beat the softened butter in a large mixing bowl until creamy.
Gradually add the confectioners' sugar, mixing well after each addition.
10. Stir in the mango puree and vanilla extract and mix until the frosting is smooth and creamy.
11. Frost the cooled cupcakes using a piping bag or spatula. Store the cupcakes in an airtight container in the refrigerator for up to 3 days.

Glazed donuts

Serves 6 donuts

Prep time: 15 minutes / Cook time: 5 minutes

Ingredients

- 120 ml warm water
- 30 ml warm milk
- 1 tsp (3g) dry active yeast
- 35g granulated sugar + 13 g
- 28g unsalted butter, melted
- Half whole egg
- Half egg yolk
- ½ tsp (2ml) vanilla extract
- 160g all-purpose flour
- Small pinch of salt
- Cooking spray
- Glaze
- 120g powdered sugar
- 30 ml milk
- 7 ml golden syrup
- ¾ tsp (3ml) vanilla extract

Preparation instructions

1. In a large measuring cup, add warm water, warm milk (45C), dry active yeast, and 13g of granulated sugar. Let the yeast mixture froth up and rise for about 5 minutes.

2. Now in a stand mixer, add the remaining of granulated sugar, unsalted melted butter, egg, egg yolk, vanilla extract, all-purpose flour (spooned and leveled off), and salt. Then pour in the yeast mixture and pace the hook attachment on and begin mixing on low speed until the flour is incorporated into liquids.

3. Next, increase the speed to high and beat for 5 minutes, and scrape down the sides of the beater bowl. If the dough looks too sticky, add 1 tablespoon of flour at a time. Make sure to mix well and scrape down the sides of the bowl between each addition of flour. (Don't add too much flour or the donuts will be too dry. They should have a slightly sticky texture to them).

4. Now place the dough in a large greased bowl and cover with a kitchen towel or plastic wrap. Let the dough rise for about one hour or until it doubles in size.

5. When the dough is ready, punch it down to release air bubbles and transfer it to a floured surface.

6. Using a rolling pin, roll the dough out to about 1. 5 cm in thickness, and using a donut cutter cut out as many donuts as you can. Then reshape the scraps and cut out some more donuts.

7. Now place the cut-out donuts on a baking sheet lined with parchment paper then cover them lightly and let them rise again for about 20-30 minutes.

8. Preheat your air fryer to 175 C and spray the air fryer basket with cooking spray and place a few donuts into the air fryer basket and spray them with some more cooking spray. Make sure that the donuts are not touching.

9. Air-fry the donuts for about 4 minutes, and repeat this process with the remaining donuts and donut holes. Then transfer the donuts onto a plate lined with paper towels.

10. To make the glaze: In a large bowl combine sugar, milk, golden syrup, and vanilla extract. While the donuts are warm dip them in the glaze and let them set on a cooling rack. The glaze sets shinier when the donuts are hot. Enjoy!

Air Fryer Ice Cream Puff Pastry Delights

Serves 4

Prep time: 10 minutes / Cook time: 10 minutes

Ingredients

- 4 puff pastry sheets, thawed
- 1 egg, beaten
- 4 scoops of your favorite ice cream
- Powdered sugar, for dusting

Preparation instructions

1. Preheat the air fryer to 200°C.
2. Cut each puff pastry sheet into a 4-inch square.
3. Brush the beaten egg on the edges of each square.
4. Place a scoop of ice cream in the center of each square.
5. Fold the corners of the square towards the center, making sure to seal the edges tightly.

6. Place the pastries in the air fryer basket, leaving space between them.

7. Air fry the pastries for 8-10 minutes, or until they are golden brown and puffed up.

8. Remove the pastries from the air fryer and let them cool for a few minutes.

9. Dust the pastries with powdered sugar before serving.

10. Serve the pastries with additional ice cream, if desired.

Cinnamon Apple Yogurt Bowl

Serves 2

Prep time: 5 minutes / Cook time: 10 minutes

Ingredients

- 1 apple, cored and sliced
- 120ml plain Greek yogurt
- 2 tbsp chopped walnuts
- 1 tbsp honey

Preparation instructions

1. Preheat the air fryer to 180°C.

2. Place the sliced apples in the air fryer basket and air fry for 5-7 minutes, or until the apples are tender and lightly browned.

3. In a mixing bowl, combine the air fried apple slices, Greek yogurt, and chopped walnuts.

4. Drizzle honey over the mixture and stir to combine.

5. Divide the mixture evenly into two serving bowls.

6. Enjoy immediately, or cover and refrigerate until ready to serve.

Decadent Chocolate Nut Pie

Serves 8

Prep time: 15 minutes / Cook time: 50 minutes

Ingredients

- 1 unbaked 9-inch pie crust
- 113g butter, melted
- 200g granulated sugar
- 60g all-purpose flour
- 2 eggs, beaten
- 25gcocoa powder
- 60ml milk
- 1 tsp vanilla extract
- 113g chopped pecans
- Whipped cream or vanilla ice cream, for serving (optional)

Preparation instructions

1. Preheat the air fryer to 180°C.

2. Place the pie crust in a 9-inch pie dish and set aside.

3. In a mixing bowl, combine the melted butter, granulated sugar, all-purpose flour, beaten eggs, cocoa powder, milk, and vanilla extract. Stir until well combined.

4. Add the chopped pecans to the mixture and stir again.

5. Pour the mixture into the pie crust.

6. Bake for 50 minutes or until the filling is set.

7. Remove from the oven and let cool for at least 15 minutes before serving.

8. Serve with whipped cream or vanilla ice cream, if desired.

9. You can also use other nuts like walnuts or almonds instead of pecans.

Brown Sugar Banana Bread

Serves 4

Prep time: 20 minutes / Cook time: 22-24 minutes

Ingredients

- 195 g packed light brown sugar
- 1 large egg, beaten
- 2 tablespoons unsalted butter, melted
- 120 ml milk, whole or semi-skimmed
- 250 g plain flour
- 1½ teaspoons baking powder
- 1 teaspoon ground cinnamon
- ½ teaspoon salt
- 1 banana, mashed
- 1 to 2 tablespoons coconut, or avocado oil oil
- 30 g icing sugar (optional)

Preparation instructions

1. In a large bowl, stir together the brown sugar, egg, melted butter, and milk.
2. In a medium bowl, whisk the flour, baking powder, cinnamon, and salt until blended. Add the flour mixture to the sugar mixture and stir just to blend.
3. Add the mashed banana and stir to combine.
4. Preheat the air fryer to 176ºC. Spritz 2 mini loaf pans with oil.
5. Evenly divide the batter between the prepared pans and place them in the air fryer basket.
6. Cook for 22 to 24 minutes, or until a knife inserted into the middle of the loaves comes out clean.
7. Dust the warm loaves with icing sugar (if using).

Blueberry Lemon Bars

Serves 8

Prep time: 10 minutes / Cook time: 20 minutes

Ingredients

- For the crust:
- 100 g almond flour
- 50 g coconut flour
- 60 ml coconut oil
- 2 tbsp honey
- For the filling:
- 2 large eggs
- Juice and zest of 1 lemon
- 50 g coconut flour
- 150 g fresh blueberries
- 1 tbsp honey

Preparation instructions

1. Preheat the air fryer to 180°C.
2. Mix almond flour, coconut flour, coconut oil and honey together until well combined.
3. Line a baking dish with baking paper.
4. Press the crust mixture evenly onto the bottom of the baking dish.
5. Bake crust in air fryer at 180°C for 5 - 8 minutes.
6. In a separate bowl, mix eggs, lemon juice, lemon zest, coconut flour and honey together until well combined.
7. Fold in blueberries.
8. Pour the filling onto the baked crust.
9. Bake in air fryer at 180°C for 15 - 20 minutes.
10. Let cool before slicing into 8 bars.

Blueberry Cream Cheese Bread Pudding

Serves 6

Prep time: 15 minutes / Cook time: 1h10 minutes

Ingredients

- 240 ml single cream
- 4 large eggs
- 65 g granulated sugar, plus 3 tablespoons
- 1 teaspoon pure lemon extract
- 4 to 5 croissants, cubed
- 150 g blueberries
- 110 g cream cheese, cut into small cubes

Preparation instructions

1. In a large bowl, combine the cream, eggs, 65 g of sugar, and the extract. Whisk until well combined. Add the cubed croissants, blueberries, and cream cheese. Toss gently until everything is thoroughly combined; set aside.
2. Place a 3-cup Bundt pan (a tube or Angel Food cake pan would work too) in the air fryer basket. Preheat the air fryer to 204°C.
3. Sprinkle the remaining 3 tablespoons sugar in the bottom of the hot pan. Cook for 10 minutes, or until the sugar caramelizes. Tip the pan to spread the caramel evenly across the bottom of the pan.
4. Remove the pan from the air fryer and pour in the bread mixture, distributing it evenly across the pan. Place the pan in the air fryer basket. Set the air fryer to 176°C and bake for 60 minutes, or until the custard is set in the middle. Let stand for 10 minutes before unmolding onto a serving plate.

Lemon Olive Oil Cake

Serves 8

Prep time: 15 minutes / Cook time: 45-50 minutes

Ingredients

- 220g all-purpose flour
- 200g sugar
- 1/2 teaspoon baking powder
- 1/2 teaspoon baking soda
- 1/2 teaspoon salt
- 3 large eggs
- 240ml extra-virgin olive oil
- 240ml whole milk
- 2 tablespoons lemon zest
- 2 tablespoons fresh lemon juice
- Powdered sugar, for dusting

Preparation instructions

1. Preheat the air fryer to 180°C and grease a 9-inch round cake pan with olive oil.
2. In a mixing bowl, whisk together flour, sugar, baking powder, baking soda, and salt.
3. In another mixing bowl, whisk together eggs, olive oil, milk, lemon zest, and lemon juice.
4. Gradually stir the dry Ingredients into the wet Ingredients until the batter is smooth.
5. Pour the batter into the prepared cake pan. Bake for 45-50 minutes or until a toothpick inserted into the center of the cake comes out clean.
6. Allow the cake to cool in the pan for 10 minutes, then transfer it to a wire rack to cool completely.
7. Dust the top of the cake with powdered sugar before serving.
8. Serve the cake at room temperature, garnished with fresh berries or whipped cream, if desired.

Air Fryer Banana Pies

Serves 4

Prep time: 10 minutes / Cook time: 10-12 minutes

Ingredients

- 2 ripe bananas, mashed
- 50g caster sugar
- 1/2 teaspoon ground cinnamon
- 1/4 teaspoon ground nutmeg
- 1/4 teaspoon salt
- 15g unsalted butter, melted
- 2 tablespoons plain flour
- 4 individual pie crusts

Preparation instructions

1. In a bowl, mix together the mashed bananas, caster sugar, cinnamon, nutmeg, salt, and melted butter until well combined.
2. Add the flour to the banana mixture and stir until the flour is fully incorporated.
3. Roll out each pie crust and cut into circles that will fit inside the air fryer basket.
4. Place each pie crust circle into the air fryer basket, pressing down lightly to fit.
5. Fill each pie crust with an equal amount of the banana mixture, spreading it evenly.
6. Cook the banana pies in the air fryer at 180°C for 10-12 minutes, or until the crust is golden brown and the filling is set.
7. Serve the banana pies warm with whipped cream or ice cream, if desired.

Air Fried Lemon Pound Cake

Serves 8

Prep time: 15 minutes / Cook time:25-30 minutes

Ingredients

- 180g all-purpose flour
- 1 teaspoon baking powder
- 1/4 teaspoon salt
- 113g unsalted butter, softened
- 200g granulated sugar
- 2 large eggs
- 120ml whole milk
- 60ml fresh lemon juice
- 2 tablespoons lemon zest

Preparation instructions

1. Preheat the air fryer to 160°C.
2. Grease a 6-inch baking pan and set aside.
3. In a bowl, whisk together the flour, baking powder, and salt.
4. In a separate bowl, beat the butter and sugar together until light and fluffy.
5. Add the eggs, one at a time, beating well after each addition.
6. Gradually stir in the flour mixture, alternating with the milk.
7. Fold in the lemon juice and lemon zest.
8. Pour the batter into the greased baking pan and smooth the surface.
9. Place the baking pan in the air fryer basket and air fry for 25-30 minutes until a toothpick inserted in the center comes out clean.
10. Remove the baking pan from the air fryer and let the pound cake cool for 10 minutes before slicing and serving.

Air fried beignets

Serves 6

Prep time: 25 minutes / Cook time:8-10 minutes

Ingredients

- 250g all-purpose flour
- 2 tablespoons granulated sugar
- 1 tablespoon active dry yeast

- 1/4 teaspoon salt
- 120ml whole milk
- 57g unsalted butter, melted
- 1 large egg
- 1 teaspoon vanilla extract
- Cooking spray
- Powdered sugar, for dusting

Preparation instructions

1. In a large mixing bowl, whisk together the flour, sugar, yeast, and salt.
2. In a separate bowl, whisk together the milk, melted butter, egg, and vanilla extract.
3. Pour the wet ingredients into the dry ingredients and stir until well combined.
4. Cover the dough with a damp cloth and let it rest for 10-15 minutes.
5. Preheat the air fryer to 180°C.
6. Lightly coat the air fryer basket with cooking spray.
7. On a floured surface, roll the dough into small balls, about 1-2 inches in diameter.
8. Place the dough balls in the air fryer basket, making sure to leave enough space between them.
9. Air fry for 8-10 minutes until golden brown and cooked through.
10. Remove the beignets from the air fryer and let them cool for a few minutes before dusting them with powdered sugar.

Air-fried churros with chocolate dipping sauce

Serves 4-6

Prep time: 15 minutes / Cook time: 8-10 minutes

Ingredients
- 125g all-purpose flour
- 50g granulated sugar
- 1/4 teaspoon salt
- 57g unsalted butter
- 240ml water
- 1/2 teaspoon vanilla extract
- 2 large eggs
- Cooking spray
- 85g semisweet chocolate chips
- 60ml heavy cream

Preparation instructions

1. In a medium saucepan, combine the butter, water, sugar, and salt. Heat over medium heat, stirring occasionally, until the butter has melted and the mixture comes to a boil.
2. Remove the saucepan from heat and add the flour, stirring constantly until the mixture comes together and forms a ball.
3. Beat in the eggs one at a time, stirring until the mixture is smooth.
4. Preheat the air fryer to 180°C.
5. Lightly coat the air fryer basket with cooking spray.
6. Fill a piping bag fitted with a star-shaped tip with the churro batter.
7. Pipe the churro batter into the air fryer basket, making long churros, leaving enough space between them.
8. Air fry for 8-10 minutes until golden brown.
9. Meanwhile, make the chocolate dipping sauce. In a microwave-safe bowl, heat the chocolate chips and heavy cream in the microwave for 30 seconds at a time, stirring in between, until the chocolate is melted and the mixture is smooth.
10. Serve the churros hot with the chocolate dipping sauce.

Air-fried strawberry shortcake

Serves 4

Prep time: 15 minutes / Cook time: 8-10 minutes

Ingredients

- 2 tbsp honey
- 125g all-purpose flour
- 50g granulated sugar
- 1/4 teaspoon salt
- 1/2 teaspoon baking powder
- 1/4 teaspoon baking soda
- 57g unsalted butter, chilled and cut into small pieces
- 120ml buttermilk
- 1 teaspoon vanilla extract
- 1 tablespoon heavy cream
- 1 tablespoon coarse sugar
- 150g fresh strawberries, sliced
- Whipped cream, for serving

Preparation instructions

1. Preheat the air fryer to 180°C.
2. In a medium bowl, whisk together the flour, sugar, salt, baking powder, and baking soda.
3. Using a pastry blender or your fingers, cut the butter into the flour mixture until it resembles coarse crumbs.
4. Stir in the buttermilk and vanilla extract until a dough forms.
5. Preheat the air fryer to 180°C.
6. Lightly grease the air fryer basket.
7. Roll out the dough on a floured surface to a thickness of about 1 inch (2.5cm).
8. Use a round cookie cutter to cut out 3-4 rounds.
9. Brush the tops of the rounds with heavy cream and sprinkle with coarse sugar.
10. Place the rounds in the air fryer basket and air fry for 8-10 minutes, or until golden brown.
11. Let the shortcakes cool slightly before slicing in half and topping with sliced strawberries and whipped cream.

Air-fried funnel cake

Serves 2-3

Prep time: 10 minutes / Cook time: 4-6 minutes

Ingredients

- 125g all-purpose flour
- 1 teaspoon baking powder
- 1/4 teaspoon salt
- 50g granulated sugar
- 120ml milk
- 1 large egg
- 1 teaspoon vanilla extract
- Powdered sugar, for dusting

Preparation instructions

1. n a medium bowl, whisk together the flour, baking powder, salt, and granulated sugar.
2. In another bowl, whisk together the milk, egg, and vanilla extract.
3. Add the wet ingredients to the dry ingredients and whisk until smooth.
4. Preheat the air fryer to 180°C.
5. Lightly grease the air fryer basket.
6. Pour the batter into a squeeze bottle with a small round tip.
7. Squeeze the batter in a swirling motion into the air fryer basket to make 2-3 funnel cakes at a time.
8. Air fry for 4-6 minutes, or until golden brown and crispy.
9. Use a spatula to carefully remove the funnel cakes from the air fryer basket and transfer to a serving plate.
10. Dust with powdered sugar and serve immediately.

Air Fried Peanut Butter Cookies

Serves 12-15 cookies

Prep time: 20 minutes / Cook time: 6-8 minutes

Ingredients
- 113g unsalted butter, softened
- 128g creamy peanut butter
- 100g granulated sugar
- 100g brown sugar
- 1 large egg
- 1 teaspoon vanilla extract
- 156g all-purpose flour
- 1/2 teaspoon baking powder
- 1/2 teaspoon baking soda
- 1/4 teaspoon salt

Preparation instructions
1. In a large bowl, cream together the butter, peanut butter, granulated sugar, and brown sugar until light and fluffy.
2. Beat in the egg and vanilla extract.
3. In a separate bowl, whisk together the flour, baking powder, baking soda, and salt.
4. Gradually mix the dry ingredients into the wet ingredients until fully combined.
5. Preheat the air fryer to 180°C.
6. Line the air fryer basket with parchment paper.
7. Roll the cookie dough into balls (about 1 tablespoon each) and place them onto the lined basket, leaving some space between them.
8. Flatten the cookie dough balls slightly with a fork.
9. Air fry for 6-8 minutes, or until the cookies are golden brown and slightly firm to the touch.
10. Use a spatula to carefully remove the cookies from the air fryer basket and transfer to a wire rack to cool completely.

Air Fried Angel Food Cake

Serves 4

Prep time: 10 minutes / Cook time: 10 minutes

Ingredients
- 120g cake flour
- 300g granulated sugar
- 1/4 teaspoon salt
- 12 large egg whites
- 1 teaspoon cream of tartar
- 1 teaspoon vanilla extract

Preparation instructions
1. Preheat the air fryer to 160°C.
2. In a large mixing bowl, sift together the cake flour, 3/4 cup of the granulated sugar, and salt.
3. In a separate mixing bowl, beat the egg whites on medium speed until frothy.
4. Add the cream of tartar and continue to beat the egg whites until soft peaks form.
5. Gradually add in the remaining 3/4 cup of granulated sugar, about 1 tablespoon at a time, while continuing to beat the egg whites on medium speed.
6. Increase the speed to high and beat the egg whites until stiff peaks form.
7. Gently fold the flour mixture into the egg whites, about 1/4 cup at a time, until fully combined.
8. Transfer the angel food cake batter to an ungreased 7-inch angel food cake pan.
9. Air fry the angel food cake for 30-35 minutes, or until a toothpick inserted into the center comes out clean.
10. Invert the angel food cake pan onto a wire rack and let it cool completely before removing the cake from the pan.

Margherita Pizza

Serves 2-3

Prep time: 5 minutes / Cook time: 8-10minutes

Ingredients

- 1 ready-made pizza crust
- 2 tbsp tomato sauce
- 1 cup shredded mozzarella cheese
- 4-5 fresh basil leaves, chopped
- Salt and black pepper to taste
- Olive oil for brushing

Preparation instructions

1. Preheat the air fryer to 180°C.
2. Place the pizza crust in the air fryer basket and brush with olive oil.
3. Spread the tomato sauce over the crust, leaving a small border around the edges.
4. Sprinkle shredded mozzarella cheese over the tomato sauce.
5. Season with salt and black pepper, to taste.
6. Place the chopped basil leaves on top of the cheese.
7. Cook the pizza in the air fryer for 8-10 minutes, or until the cheese is melted and bubbly.
8. Slice and serve hot.

Vegetarian Pizza

Serves 2-3

Prep time: 10 minutes / Cook time: 8-10 minutes

Ingredients

- 1 ready-made pizza crust
- 60ml pizza sauce
- 50g shredded mozzarella cheese
- 30g sliced black olives
- 30g sliced bell peppers
- 30g sliced mushrooms
- Salt and black pepper to taste
- Olive oil for brushing

Preparation instructions

1. Preheat the air fryer to 180°C.
2. Place the pizza crust in the air fryer basket and brush with olive oil.
3. Spread the pizza sauce over the crust, leaving a small border around the edges.
4. Sprinkle shredded mozzarella cheese over the pizza sauce.
5. Add the sliced black olives, bell peppers, and mushrooms on top of the cheese.
6. Season with salt and black pepper, to taste.
7. Cook the pizza in the air fryer for 8-10 minutes, or until the cheese is melted and bubbly.
8. Slice and serve hot.

Meat Lover's Pizza

Serves 4

Prep time: 15 minutes / Cook time: 8-10 minutes

Ingredients

- 1 ready-made pizza crust
- 60 ml pizza sauce
- 100 g shredded mozzarella cheese
- 30 g sliced pepperoni
- 30 g cooked sausage, crumbled
- 30 g cooked bacon, crumbled

- Salt and black pepper to taste
- Olive oil for brushing

Preparation instructions

1. Preheat the air fryer to 180°C.
2. Place the pizza crust in the air fryer basket and brush with olive oil.
3. Spread the pizza sauce over the crust, leaving a small border around the edges.
4. Sprinkle shredded mozzarella cheese over the pizza sauce.
5. Add the sliced pepperoni, crumbled sausage, and crumbled bacon on top of the cheese.
6. Season with salt and black pepper, to taste.
7. Cook the pizza in the air fryer for 8-10 minutes, or until the cheese is melted and bubbly.
8. Slice and serve hot.

BBQ Pulled Vegetarian Wrap

Serves 2

Prep time: 10 minutes / Cook time: 5-7 minutes

Ingredients

- 240g chickpeas, drained and rinsed
- 120ml BBQ sauce
- 1/2 red onion, chopped
- 1/2 green bell pepper, chopped
- 1/2 red bell pepper, chopped
- 2 large flour tortillas
- 30g shredded cheddar cheese
- Salt and black pepper to taste

Preparation instructions

1. Preheat the air fryer to 200°C.
2. In a bowl, mash the chickpeas with a fork or potato masher until they are broken down but still chunky.

3. Add BBQ sauce, chopped red onion, green and red bell peppers, salt, and black pepper. Mix well.
4. Divide the mixture evenly between the two flour tortillas.
5. Top each tortilla with 2 tbsp of shredded cheddar cheese.
6. Roll up each tortilla and place them seam side down in the air fryer basket.
7. Cook for 5-7 minutes, or until the tortillas are golden brown and the cheese is melted.
8. Serve hot.

Chicken Fajita Wrap

Serves 4

Prep time: 5 minutes / Cook time: 10-12 minutes

Ingredients

- 4 tortilla wraps
- 200g of sliced chicken breast
- 100g of sliced peppers
- 100g of sliced onions
- 2 tablespoons of olive oil
- 1 teaspoon of chili powder
- 1 teaspoon of cumin powder
- Salt and pepper, to taste

Preparation instructions

1. Preheat the air fryer to 180 °C.
2. In a mixing bowl, combine the sliced chicken, peppers, onions, olive oil, chili powder, cumin powder, salt, and pepper. Mix until well combined.
3. Place the chicken and vegetable mixture in the air fryer and cook for 8-10 minutes or until the chicken is cooked through and the vegetables are tender, flipping halfway

through.

4. Remove from the air fryer and let it cool for a few minutes before serving.

5. Place the cooked chicken and vegetables in the center of each tortilla wrap and roll them up tightly.

6. Place the wraps in the air fryer and cook for 2-3 minutes or until the tortilla is golden brown and crispy.

Pepperoni Pizza Dip

Serves 6

Prep time: 10 minutes / Cook time: 10 minutes

Ingredients

- 170 g soft white cheese
- 177 ml shredded Italian cheese blend
- 60 ml sour cream
- 1½ teaspoons dried Italian seasoning
- ¼ teaspoon garlic salt
- ¼ teaspoon onion powder
- 177 ml pizza sauce
- 120 ml sliced miniature pepperoni
- 60 ml sliced black olives
- 1 tablespoon thinly sliced green onion
- Cut-up raw vegetables, toasted baguette slices, pitta chips, or tortilla chips, for serving

Preparation instructions

1. In a small bowl, combine the soft white cheese, 60 ml of the shredded cheese, the sour cream, Italian seasoning, garlic salt, and onion powder. Stir until smooth and the Ingredients are well blended.

2. Spread the mixture in a baking pan. Top with the pizza sauce, spreading to the edges. Sprinkle with the remaining 120 ml shredded

cheese. Arrange the pepperoni slices on top of the cheese. Top with the black olives and green onion.

3. Place the pan in the air fryer basket. Set the air fryer to 176°C for 10 minutes, or until the pepperoni is beginning to brown on the edges and the cheese is bubbly and lightly browned.

4. Let stand for 5 minutes before serving with vegetables, toasted baguette slices, pitta chips, or tortilla chips.

Cheesy Pepperoni and Chicken Pizza

Serves 6

Prep time: 15 minutes / Cook time: 15 minutes

Ingredients

- 280 g cooked chicken, cubed
- 240 g pizza sauce
- 20 slices pepperoni
- 20 g grated Parmesan cheese
- 225 g shredded Mozzarella cheese
- Cooking spray

Preparation instructions

1. Preheat the air fryer to 190°C. Spritz a baking pan with cooking spray.

2. Arrange the chicken cubes in the prepared baking pan, then top the cubes with pizza sauce and pepperoni. Stir to coat the cubes and pepperoni with sauce.

3. Scatter the cheeses on top, then place the baking pan in the preheated air fryer. Air fryer for 15 minutes or until frothy and the cheeses melt

4. Serve

Printed in Great Britain
by Amazon

20517184R00052